A Legacy of Church Planting

Robert D. Miller

CROSS
BOOKS

CrossBooks
1663 Liberty Drive
Bloomington, IN 47403
www.crossbooks.com

First published by CrossBooks   5/4/2009

ISBN: 978-1-6150-7032-9 (sc)

Printed in the United States of America
Bloomington, Indiana

This book is printed on acid-free paper.

Contents

Foreword

I'm often asked, "What was it like growing up with Jerry Falwell as your dad?" That is indeed an interesting question. And, there are many answers I could give when confronted with such inquiries. But, one thing is certain: I had the privilege of growing up surrounded by heroes, with my Dad being my greatest hero. Because of Dad's spiritual leadership in culture and politics, I met many amazing people like Presidents Ronald Reagan, George H.W. Bush, George W. Bush, Sen. Ted Kennedy, Bob Hope, Peter Jennings of ABC News, Tom Brokaw of NBC News, CNN host Larry King, Dallas Cowboys head coach Tom Landry, NFL Hall of Famers Art Monk and Darrell Green, NFL great Steve Bartkowski and many other "heroes" of the American culture. It was fascinating to come in contact with these cultural icons through the years.

However, I ultimately realized that I really didn't have to look far to see real heroes in action. They were all around me at Thomas Road Baptist Church and Liberty University. Many courageous men and women came through our church and the university Dad founded with the purpose of preparing church planters to answer God's call. You may be thinking, "Wait a minute, Church planters are heroes?"

Absolutely!

These believers step out in faith, blaze trails for others, leave all the comforts of home, sacrifice for God's greater purpose and do all they can to reach souls with the Gospel. They know that the local church is God's master plan for local and world evangelization. And they participate in this plan without reservation. That's what heroes do!

Most often, these brothers and sisters in Christ work tirelessly toward the vision God has given them without expecting accolades or recognition. It is often a thankless job that they take on. That's why I'm glad my friend Bob Miller has gathered this collection of inspiring stories about some of the most effective church planters I have ever known -- people who are true heroes.

The pastors in this book were each encouraged and inspired in some way by my Dad's own vision for church planting. Their heroic efforts span thirty years of church planting across America.

I pray their stories will inspire you to greater ministry. I hope they will cause you to rethink your own calling from God and your work for Him. Further, I pray that these stories may help challenge some to take up the vision of planting churches and becoming true heroes of the faith.

- *Jonathan Falwell*
Senior Pastor, Thomas Road Baptist Church
Executive Vice President of Spiritual Affairs, Liberty University

"It was 50 years ago.

I was a 22-year-old recent Bible college graduate, returning to my hometown, Lynchburg, Virginia,

to plant a new church

and capture a city for Christ."

Pastor Jerry Falwell
An Incredible Journey
2006

Acknowledgments

I want to acknowledge the thirty-plus-year influence of my friend, pastor, mentor, and counselor, the late Dr. Jerry Falwell. Thank you for your vision, faith, and commitment to your community. Additional thanks to Dr. Elmer Towns; you encouraged me to write this book and shared e-mails with many great suggestions.

To another friend, pastor, and church leader, thank you, Jonathan Falwell, for your encouragement and contribution. I will go to the Throne of Grace for you each and every Sunday morning.

Thank you to Shelly Roark and Peter Roark for editing and creative thoughts. Thank you to Doug Randlett for supporting this project. Thank you to Daniel, Justin, Vernon, Rick, Scott and also those who pray on Sunday morning with me. Thank you to Polly, for your faithful support over these past years. Special thanks to Rusty, my dear friend, business partner and sounding board.

Thank you to my mom and dad, Bob and Kate Miller, for giving me so many great opportunities—especially Liberty—and to Debi's parents, Ed and Ethel Ivins … thank you.

Special thanks to my wonderful wife and love of my life, Debi. Thank you for your support and commitment to all that I do. I love you.

Also, thank you to my children who have prayed for me, encouraged me, and bragged about me during this process: Andrea and Brandon Webb, Alyssa and Jason Pantana, Amanda and Kenny Pate, and Alydia.

And to Bentley (and all the forthcoming grandchildren) ... the next generation of Kingdom building is yours. Be faithful, be obedient, and be courageous.

Introduction

May 15, 2007, is one of the days I will never forget. It was our twenty-fifth wedding anniversary. Debi and I had plans for lunch and were going to spend the afternoon together.

While in my office, I received a late-morning call telling me Dr. Falwell had been rushed to the hospital. He was unresponsive, and his condition looked serious. After making a couple of calls, we discovered that what we had all feared had become reality: Dr. Jerry Falwell had passed on to eternity.

I called Debi and tearfully told her what had happened. She met me at my office, and we went to lunch. I don't remember what we ate, but I do remember we talked about Dr. Falwell and his influence on our lives.

We decided to put the rest of our plans on hold. Instead, we drove up to the Liberty University monogram that sits on a ridge of Liberty Mountain.

As we neared the top of the ridge, we saw the entire campus of Liberty and Thomas Road Baptist Church. Within moments, I was flooded with memories of what God had done for the past fifty years through this incredible ministry.

Jerry's ministry was life-changing. It was moving, it was touching, it was full of faith and full of vision—and we were privileged to have been a part of it.

That day, I began to see the influence and reach of Dr. Falwell's life in a different way. He did not touch just a church and its far-reaching ministries. It was not just about a Christian educational system that is the largest in the world. Instead, I began to view his life as a perpetual passing of the torch from one young champion to the next, as one changed life touching another changed life, and as one generation giving rise to the next generation.

Jerry Falwell, through the grace of God and a visionary faith that could move mountains, left a ministry that will affect generation upon generation upon generation. It will continue to live in the lives of those who have walked this faith campus.

Paul told Timothy in the last of his recorded writings, "And the things you have heard of me in the presence of many witnesses, the same commit to faithful men who shall be able to teach others, also" (2 Timothy 2:2).

Dr. Falwell took this admonition to heart.

This book is a narrative of the legacy and impact of Dr. Falwell's ministry on a very select group of individuals who were infused with the dynamics of doing what he did for the Kingdom of God: planting a church and capturing a city for Christ.

Throughout this book, you will find story after story of men and women who have heeded the mandate of Dr. Falwell and gone out to plant churches.

I know most of those whose stories are told in this book. I have heard them preach and heard them teach. I have worked with several. I have taught some. I have prayed with many. I admire them all.

Some I have known for just a few months; many I have known for years, some for more than thirty years.

These men are my heroes and I thank God for Carl, David, Danny, Andy, Chris W., Matt, Brian, Mark, Randy, Jimmy, Tim, Chris R., and Vernon. They are just a few of hundreds who have gone out and planted churches and are part of this legacy.

From various parts of the country, from different denominational networks and organizations, given to diverse styles of worship and praise, the churches represented here share two common bonds: they all had a powerful, defining moment at Thomas Road Baptist Church or Liberty University, and they are all reaching their communities.

Thank you, Lord Jesus, that You are building Your church, and the gates of hell will never prevail!

Chapter 1
A Humble Beginning

"What God's Spirit can accomplish in this world is far greater than anything we could ever do. Taking time out from our busy, self-appointed agendas to wait upon the Lord, to praise, honor, and love Him sets free His power to get done what we could only dream."

- Dr. Jerry Falwell

Story

In the spring of 1956, Helen Falwell watched her twenty-two-year-old son graduate from Bible college. It was what she had hoped for, but she could hardly believe it was happening. For years she had tuned in every Sunday to Dr. Charles E. Fuller's radio broadcast, the *Old-Fashioned Revival Hour*. She prayed very hard for her son's conversion. And only four years earlier, he had gone to a small Baptist church on a cold Sunday evening, recognized the familiar radio style of preaching, felt the conviction of God's Spirit, and met his Savior. Now she was watching him graduate, called as a pastor. It was one of the greatest highlights of her life.

Her son Jerry was ready to plant a church in Macon, Georgia. He had been tested and tried as a young leader and convinced of his calling to shepherd a church. Before embarking on this new journey, he wanted to spend some time at home in Lynchburg, Virginia.

In 1817, Thomas Jefferson penned these words about Lynchburg: "I consider it as the most interesting spot in the State, and the most entitled to general patronage for its industry, enterprise and correct course."[1] Little did Jerry Falwell know how this "interesting spot" would determine the "correct course" for his life.

While at home, young Falwell was asked to preach in Richmond for two weeks for a vacationing pastor. But while Jerry was preaching there, a familiar church in Lynchburg faced difficulties.

Park Avenue Baptist Church was where Jerry, along with some of his friends, had heard the stirring message that led to their conversions. Jerry often took time from school to help with the various ministries of the church. The church grew to appreciate his gifts and heart for ministry.

In the early summer of 1956, Park Avenue began to face challenges with an interim pastor. Consequently, thirty-five members decided to leave. These members felt as if they had been run out of their own church. Many had been founding members of the church. They were devastated and overcome with a sense of hopelessness. Several of the men planned to start another church; they had done it before, and they could do it again.

As they discussed the formation of a new church, young Jerry Falwell's name came up as a potential pastor. These churchless saints drove to Richmond and met with Falwell to discuss it.

As they explained what happened, Jerry Falwell's patient and encouraging response was that of a wise leader. He reminded them of his plans to go to Macon and plant a church there. But, prompted in his heart, he also told them he would pray and ask God for direction.

In all of his education and training, Jerry had never faced this issue. It would require an intense time of prayer.

He remembered the time in Bible college when he had faced failure over a Sunday school class for eleven-year-old boys. No matter how hard he tried, no matter how good his lessons, no matter how much he wanted to succeed, he could not make that class grow. He was a disappointment to the Sunday school superintendent and to himself.

---

1   Dorothy T. and Clifford W. Potter, *Lynchburg: "The Most Interesting Spot"* (Lynchburg, Va.: Progress Publishing Corp, 1976)

It was in that desperation that Jerry found an empty room in the dormitory and every afternoon began to cry out to God, asking Him for grace and direction. God gave him peace, and his class began to grow. Expressing dependence upon God through prayer and petition grew into a wellspring of strength in the life of Jerry Falwell.

Prayer clarified the need of the moment and the consequences in eternity. In later years, Jerry would often be quoted as saying, "All failures are prayer failures." He learned how to pray and learned the power of prayer.

Jerry contacted those who were interested in starting the new church and stated, "I believe the Lord wants me to stay here and help you build this church."[2]

In an effort to influence the community for good, Falwell requested a meeting with his friend, Pastor Woods of Park Avenue Baptist Church. Jerry's desire was that both congregations could work together in a spirit of peace and brotherly love. He stated that they should "pray and work together and both churches will grow."[3]

Both men agreed with the harmonious solution. Pastor Woods asked to confer with the Baptist Bible Fellowship, an international fellowship of more than 4,000 churches and the sponsoring entity of Baptist Bible College, Jerry's alma mater.

In its judgment, the BBF decreed that the saints who had left Park Avenue were dissenters and had created an insurgence. The ruling stated that Falwell's association with the new church was an act of compliance with the dissenters, and he was mandated to "cease and desist."

Their ultimatum to young Falwell:

If you do not leave Lynchburg immediately, you will be cut off from the Baptist Bible Fellowship International. You will not be welcome to preach in our churches or attend our fellowship meetings. We will not

---

2   Macel Falwell, *Jerry Falwell: His Life and Legacy* (: Howard Books 2008), page 38

3   Ibid, page 38

accept students from your church nor will our students be allowed to assist you in your ministry.[4]

Jerry faced a dilemma, the first of many he would encounter in his ministry: Obey God, who had confirmed His direction through prayer, or yield and align with those who had been his mentors, teachers, and leaders. Consistent with his character, Jerry Falwell chose to "obey God rather than men". (Acts 5:29)

This was the first of many steps of faith for Jerry. He would later be quoted as saying, "Faith is learning to live without an explanation." This situation had no reasonable explanation.

Macel Falwell writes in her book, *Jerry Falwell: His Life and Legacy*, "When Jerry looked back over his life, he cited this experience as the most painful thing he'd ever endured. He was 22 years old and had been a Christian for only four years."[5]

Jerry was confident he had heard from God. With no preview meetings, a limited strategy, a congregation of wounded saints who trusted God, and no experience in church planting, Jerry Falwell began a journey that would last a lifetime.

On Sunday, June 17, 1956, a young, single, twenty-two-year-old Bible school graduate met with thirty-five adults and their children in Mountain View Elementary School and led their first services as a new, unnamed church. He preached on the Great Commission and prophetically vowed, "We will reach the lost people of Lynchburg with the gospel."[6]

On the following Wednesday, Falwell and Lawson "Pop" Johnson found a potential location for Lynchburg's newest church. An old warehouse/manufacturing building on Thomas Road had housed the bankrupt Donald Duck Bottling Company. Windows were boarded up, weeds flourished on the property, and the interior still smelled of cola syrup. Yet this seemed to be the building that God would use to

---

4   Ibid, page 39
5   Ibid, page 40
6   Elmer L. Towns and Daniel Henderson, *The Church That Prays Together* (Colorado Springs: NavPress 2008), page 98

birth one of the greatest churches in America. Jerry and Pop bowed their heads and asked God to provide this building as a place for the light of Jesus to shine in a darkened world.

The next night, a group of believers held a prayer meeting in the dirty one-room cola bottling company's building.

> An organizational meeting was also conducted that evening. A formal call was given to Jerry Falwell to be the pastor of the newly-formed church, and a simple constitution and bylaws were adopted. The first three trustees were elected, and the name chosen for the church was the Thomas Road Baptist Church. Those present at that initial, foundational meeting voted unanimously to designate one tenth of the church's offerings to missions.[7]

The following Sunday, June 24, 1956, the first church service was held in the newly cleaned Thomas Road facility. Falwell led the music and preached. Macel Pate, soon to be Jerry's wife, played the piano.

Strategy

Jerry immediately claimed Acts 1:8 as his "Master Strategy Plan" for Lynchburg: "But ye shall receive power, after that the Holy Ghost is come upon you: and ye shall be witnesses unto me both in Jerusalem, and in all Judaea, and in Samaria, and unto the uttermost part of the earth." His "Jerusalem" was the ten-block radius surrounding the current church location. His "Judaea" included an expanded twenty-block radius. His "Samaria" was the remaining city of Lynchburg, and his "uttermost parts of the earth" was the surrounding three counties. Little did Jerry Falwell know that this ministry would literally reach around the world.

Jerry would visit every house in his strategy plan. Every day, six days a week, he would knock on doors in his community: 100 doors a day, 600 doors a week. With every house, he would leave his business

---

7   Ruth McClellan, *An Incredible Journey* (Lynchburg, VA: Liberty University 2006), page 77

card and phone number. He would read the Bible with the residents, encourage them, pray with them, and invite them to the new Thomas Road Baptist Church. Jerry chose two men to go with him and get "on-the-job" training in visitation. By the second Sunday, attendance had doubled. Loving people to Christ through continuous witnessing became the spiritual foundation upon which Thomas Road Baptist Church was built.[8]

As Jerry continued to visit every home in the area, attendance grew. With the help of a volunteer, Falwell began publishing a weekly newsletter. Every Saturday afternoon, more volunteers would call each person that had been visited that week. Within a week's timeframe, visitors would receive three "touches" from TRBC.

Falwell often recalled the power of listening to the radio each Sunday morning as his mother left for church. He wondered what type of impact a daily radio program would have on his community. In September 1956, Falwell started a daily radio program called *The Deep Things of God*. This thirty-minute early morning broadcast welcomed listeners to a new day. In December, a half-hour television program began airing called *Thomas Road Baptist Church Presents*. This program was broadcast at 5:30 p.m. every Sunday. People in the area would listen to Jerry tell about God's great work on the radio, and then they would go to Thomas Road that night and experience that work of God in the church.

Through developing leaders, visitation, multiple contacts with residents, use of print media, a daily radio program, and a television broadcast each Sunday, Jerry Falwell and Thomas Road Baptist Church became a powerful presence in the community.

At its first anniversary, TRBC had an attendance of 864.

Maudena Moore was a young lady who came to find work in Lynchburg in 1957 at the Cradock and Terry Shoe Factory. She talks about the impact of Pastor Falwell and Thomas Road Baptist Church,

> We rented a room in the Rivermont area, and my
> landlady would call me downstairs every Sunday

---

8   Ibid, page 80

afternoon to watch Jerry Falwell on TV. I wanted so much to attend Thomas Road Baptist Church, but I wasn't on the bus route at that time and didn't have any transportation.

After working a few weeks, my forelady, Lucille Pate (Macel Falwell's mother) invited me and took me to TRBC's first Friend Day. I was so excited! That day was a "defining moment" in my life, as I have now been a part of the ministry for 47 years.

For years, Jerry and his family or his in-laws would pick me up and take me to church. Even after I married, if my husband was out of town, they would make sure I had a ride to church. Jerry has never been too busy for people.

I feel Jerry has made an impact and a difference because he is not afraid to speak out on issues. He shakes hands with Presidents and Prime Ministers, but he still puts his arms around the poor, the fallen, or any needy family. He has always been there for my family. That's my pastor.[9]

Under the visionary leadership and faith walking example of Pastor Jerry Falwell, the ministries of Thomas Road Baptist Church continued to grow throughout the next fifty years.

Ever expanding buildings and campuses, Elim Home for Alcoholics, *The Old-Time Gospel Hour* program, children's and youth camps, Liberty Christian Academy, Liberty University, Liberty Baptist Theological Seminary, Liberty School of Law, Liberty Home Bible Institute, Hope Aglow, the Center, World Missions, Liberty Godparent Home, Liberty Alliance, Liberty Counsel, Moral Majority Coalition—the miracle has continued to grow and reach the world.

On a cold January night in 1971, Dr. Falwell was leading the regular Wednesday night prayer meeting. His message that night would be something special. It would literally change the face of Christian

9   Ibid, page 85

education and touch the world for Christ. Falwell's text for the evening was 2 Timothy 2:2: "And the things that thou hast heard of me among many witnesses, the same commit thou to faithful men, who shall be able to teach others also." Jerry then shared these historic words,

> While He was on this earth, Jesus Christ chose 12 men to follow Him closely. Men have always been God's method for carrying the gospel to the world. Jesus' objective was to reproduce his life in men who would then bear witness of Him and carry on His work after He had returned to the Father. These 12 men shook the world for God.
>
> The Apostle Paul knew that if his ministry was to continue after the Lord called him home, it would have to be carried on by a younger person. The Bible tells us Paul committed this responsibility to a young man named Timothy.
>
> God has been very good to us. Some of you sitting here tonight remember when there was just a handful of us. We have witnessed many miracles, and to whom much is given, much is required. Because there are 4 billion people living today, there is greater need for training young Timothys now than there ever has been before in history.
>
> Young people are the hope of our nation and our world. I believe we have a sacred obligation to provide thousands of young people with a solid Christian education. Let us dedicate ourselves tonight to starting a college with the goal of seeing thousands of young men and women, deeply in love with the Lord Jesus Christ, who will go out in all walks of life to shake this world for God.[10]

That night was the conception of Lynchburg Baptist College (now known as Liberty University). Along with the development and creation

10   Ibid, pages 138-140

of a world-class university, this became the sending arm of energized, enthusiastic, called, and committed local church planters.

In 1980, Falwell continued to expand his strategy to reach the world by forming the Liberty Baptist Fellowship (LBF). LBF began as a church planting extension of the ministry of TRBC/LU. To date, they have assisted in planting over 200 churches.

Successes

Identifying the successes over a fifty-year period could get voluminous. The successes of Falwell's ministry are seen in his ability to trust and believe God no matter what the circumstances. He has been quoted as saying, "I am convinced that if we will attend to the depth of our ministry, God will attend to its breadth."

Prayer was a focal point of Jerry Falwell's life and ministry. In the earliest days of Thomas Road, prayer warriors of old like R. C. Worley, "Pop" Johnson, Percy Hall, and Sam Pate would gather in an old compressor room on a dirt floor and intercede for a young pastor and a young church.

In the early years of the church, Jerry would share visions with his congregation and then declare that only with God's help could they reach these goals. People began to pray—and God moved.

In the mid 1970s, the church or school would face a crisis, and Jerry would call the entire church to prayer and fasting. The effect on the community was so great, Jerry would receive calls from local restaurant owners asking him not to call the church to prayer and fasting because of the economic results in the community. People began to pray—and God moved.

In January 1978, Falwell began chapel for Liberty Baptist College and said, "We're cancelling our formal chapel program today. I want all of you to follow me up the hill to the seven uncompleted dorms. We'll all march around them once in faith, and then kneel in groups of seven to intercede to God for $5 million to finish them." People began to pray—and God moved.

In 1985, Jerry called the congregation of Thomas Road and the student body of Liberty to pray for then LU Vice President Vernon Brewer, who had developed cancer and had a five-pound tumor removed. Vernon's vocal cords were damaged during surgery, and the doctors thought he would never speak again. People began to pray, to fast, to trust—and God moved.

In 1997, Jerry participated in two forty-day fasts. Liberty University received a $52 million miracle. People began to pray—and God moved.

In 2003, Thomas Road Baptist had the opportunity to purchase 800,000 square feet of industrial office and warehouse space situated on 113 acres contiguous to Liberty University. This purchase would allow the ministries to rest on one piece of property. *We began to pray.* Ericsson, a major Swiss company, rejected TRBC's offer of $5 million. *But we continued to pray.* The property went to an absolute closed bid auction. TRBC bid $10.2 million and won the property. Thomas Road had until February 14, 2003, to close. *We continued to pray.*

The next day, Dr. Falwell flew to Oklahoma City to meet with David Green, owner of Hobby Lobby retail stores. A privately held company, Hobby Lobby and Mr. Green had committed themselves to spread the Gospel of Christ and expand the Kingdom. They had offered to donate a large property located in Chicago to the ministry of Liberty University. After LU concluded that the property would not be suitable for its purposes, Jerry wanted to personally and respectfully communicate the decision to Mr. Green.

In the course of conversation, Dr. Falwell told Mr. Green about the Ericsson property and the decision before Thomas Road Baptist Church. Without hesitation, Mr. Green said, "Let me buy the building and donate it to Thomas Road Baptist Church ministries." On February 19, 2003, Hobby Lobby closed on the property and leased it to TRBC at an annual rate of one dollar. A year later, the $10.55 million property of over 800,000 square feet and 113 acres was donated to the TRBC ministries. *People began to pray—and God moved.*

Dr. Falwell's commitments to prayer, his ability to trust God, and his faith walk have shaped the core values of the TRBC ministries.

Struggles

In 1973, charges by the Securities and Exchange Commission against Thomas Road Baptist Church; in 1983, an article in *Hustler* magazine satirizing Dr. Falwell and his family; in 1987, the fall of Jim Bakker and the fallout over PTL's disgrace; the failure of leadership; the loss of a daughter's marriage; the loss of loved ones—each of these was a struggle or challenge that could have caused shipwreck. Dr. Falwell's focus and trust were evident in some of his more familiar quotes.

"It always costs you something to do a work for the Lord. If it does not cost you anything, it is not worth doing. Winning is getting up earlier than the other guy and going to bed later, and it is working harder in between. I personally do not think anyone has ever hurt himself by working hard."

•••

"You do not determine a man's greatness by his talent or wealth, as the world does, but rather by what it takes to discourage him."

•••

"From time to time the stars will fall out of your heaven; your world will collapse around you. Strength and stability are born in the storms of adversity. Your reaction and response to trouble during the hours of your suffering will determine the extent to which God can effectively use your life for His glory."

•••

"Humanly, many situations may look hopeless. But we dare not look at anything humanly—we are children of the King of the Universe."

•••

"There are times when every leader must do what he believes is right, even if the cost of doing that is very high."

Significance

The ministry of Dr. Jerry Falwell, Thomas Road Baptist Church, and the Liberty University educational system have provided one of the most comprehensive local church based ministries in the world. It parallels the outreach of the early church in regard to reaching the present and future generations.

Summary

Dr. Falwell demonstrated the following characteristics of ministry:

Visionary Leadership: The ability to determine, discern, articulate, and cast a vision, by example and by creating a movement to accomplish the vision.

Trusting Faith: The ability to visualize God's direction, to believe it, to trust it, and to act upon it with complete confidence.

Strategic Outreach: The ability to systemically reach a community, a city, a nation and a world.

Ministry Longevity: The ability to plant and grow, reproducing yourself in others and perpetuating growth in others.

Family Commitment: God first, family first.

Redemptive Acceptance: God is a God of the second chance. We are all wounded soldiers, many of us with self inflicted wounds. God restores, and so must we.

Fourth Quarter Obligation: Finish Strong.

Dominating Goals: Make the goals in our ministries big, make them hairy, and make them audacious.

Social Relevance: The ability to address the current social issues of the day, from a Biblical base and a caring intent.

Borderless Outreach: There are no boundaries to doing God's work, God's way, with God's people. You must use every available means to reach every available person.

Soul

The soul of the church is the Sunday morning services. These services reach past Lynchburg into the surrounding area of central Virginia. In addition, the services are televised and carry the gospel of Jesus Christ to millions of homes across the world.

Statistics and Structure

Thomas Road Baptist Church's current sanctuary seats 5,000 and has 5,000 parking spaces. It is located on the convergence of two major Virginia expressways. Church attendance is approximately 11,000 in four Sunday services at three different venues.

Sunday school or Adult Bible Communities average more than 8,000 in attendance. Ancillary ministries include full educational programs from pre-kindergarten to doctoral programs. Additional community outreach programs also exist.

Thomas Road Baptist Church's annual budget is approximately $10 million, with more than 10 percent designated to local and foreign outreach programs. It employs more than 200 people and is affiliated with the Southern Baptist Convention. TRBC is a pastor-led church. It is supported by a deacon board.

> Our greatest value is to reproduce ourselves in the lives
> of others. When you leave behind a vibrant Christian
> who knows his calling, and his commission, you can be
> buried, but you will live on through all those in whom
> you have been reproduced.
>
> - Dr. Jerry Falwell

I will always remember him [Dr. Falwell] as a church planter whose church became one of the greatest in America. Not only that, but in his role as founder and chancellor of Liberty University, Jerry has trained up tremendous young champions for Christ who are planting churches and sharing the light of the Gospel around the world.

- Geoff Hammond
- President of SBC North American Mission Board
- On the death of Jerry Falwell, May 15, 2007

Chapter 2
Committed to God's Vision

"But the greatest lesson will be vision. The ability to think big is not learned in Bible college or seminary. We learn vision by seeing the work of God through the eyes of a man of God."

> - Dr. Elmer Towns, excerpt from *The Ten Largest Sunday Schools and What Makes Them Grow*

Story

Carl Godwin is tenacious when it comes to following God's call. He knew while he was still in high school in his hometown of Lincoln, Nebraska, that God was leading him into ministry. But it was after graduating from Bethany Nazarene College in Oklahoma City, while he was working on his master's degree, that he discovered the passion that would shape that ministry—and change his life.

That passion ignited when Carl began reading Dr. Elmer Towns' book, *The Ten Largest Sunday Schools and What Makes Them Grow.*

> Little did I realize what an impact it would have on my life. The book captivated me. I had never seen such churches like I read about in Elmer Towns' book. My home church might have an attendance of 125 people on a good day.
>
> How exciting to read about churches reaching so many for Christ and making such an impact on their communities. My experience had been to have a new pastor every two or three years, so it was a new paradigm

to learn of men, each giving his whole life to one local church.

Carl wanted to write his thesis on some of the churches featured in *The Ten Largest* book, but was denied that chance. Undaunted, Carl told his wife, Gayle, that after finishing graduate school, he wanted to spend a year studying the churches he had read about.

So after graduate school in the mid 60's, the couple moved to attend one of those churches—First Baptist of Hammond, Indiana (close to Chicago). The move also allowed them to be centrally located in order to visit the other nine churches of *The Ten Largest*.

But it wasn't easy. Carl remembers,

> We were shocked at the cost of living in Chicago. We had been paying $55 a month rent for a furnished house in Oklahoma, but anything in Chicago was four times that amount. Two hundred dollars a month rent was outrageous! After looking for five days we finally found a one bedroom unfurnished duplex in Gary, Indiana, for $160 a month. Since we had no furniture, and, thankfully, we didn't know what a credit card was, we had to be creative. Our dinette set was a card table with two trunks to sit on for chairs, and our bed was made of blankets on the floor. We did not complain though because we were excited to be started on our one-year study of what God was doing in growing churches in America.

Gayle got a job in a drugstore, and Carl began working the night shift at Youngstown Steel Mill. He worked at the garage with mechanics who kept the equipment running. When they learned Carl was preparing for the ministry, he was soon dubbed "Parson."

Carl writes,

> As the new guy I was given the jobs no one else wanted. One of these jobs was to power wash the big trucks and steel moving equipment. One night as I was power

washing a big machine, a mechanic came into the washroom and said, "Parson, rumor has it that you have already finished college and have a degree. Is that right?" I didn't tell him I had actually finished grad school and had a master's degree. I just said, "Yes, that's right." Then as he turned and walked away he said, "Then what are you doing here?"

As I went back to work, the devil put thoughts in my head like: "Is this what you went to school for? You could be a pastor right now." It was true that our year study was sometimes just a financial struggle for survival. But I reminded myself and the enemy of why we were there and that God had put it in our hearts to learn how to lead a church to reach many for Christ and make an impact on a community.

When the Godwins left Oklahoma for Chicago, another couple they knew left for Lynchburg, Virginia, to be part of Jerry Falwell's Thomas Road Baptist Church. Thomas Road was also in Elmer Towns's book *The Ten Largest*.

Carl's friends sent him an application for a teaching position in the new Lynchburg Baptist College, cofounded by Jerry Falwell and Dr. Elmer Towns in 1971. Carl said he was doubtful the college would have any interest in him but filled out the application anyway.

About the same time, Carl was offered a church staff position in Gary, Indiana. Carl says it was tempting,

After working nights in the dirty mill, a ministry opportunity sounded exciting. But after three days of prayer and fasting, God made it very clear to me that I was not to take the offer. Continuing to work at the steel mill was not appealing, but God said, "Stay the course." The very next day I got a call from Lynchburg Baptist College asking me to come for a job interview! I felt like I needed to pinch myself to see if I was dreaming. I was beside myself with excitement to get

to meet Dr. Elmer Towns, the president of the college
and, of course, the author of the best selling book that
God had used as such a catalyst to change my life.

At Lynchburg Baptist College, Carl taught four classes of English
and audited two classes under Dr. Towns. The spirit of revival at
Thomas Road Baptist Church and Lynchburg Baptist College fueled
Carl's faith and made him more determined than ever to follow the
vision God had planted within him. Carl remembers something that
Jerry often said: "The difference between greatness and mediocrity in
the work of God is vision."

Carl says that Jerry Falwell challenged him to dream big and ask
big with the confidence of Jeremiah 32:27: "Behold, I am the Lord,
the God of all flesh; is anything too difficult for Me?" (NASB 1995).

During this time, Dr. Towns was writing a series of articles for
The Sword of the Lord newspaper on great soul-winning churches in
America. Each Sunday he visited a different church to minister and
interview the pastor. Carl made several of the trips with Dr. Towns and
got to visit not only seven of the *The Ten Largest* but also several other
great, growing churches.

After spending time learning the principles of church growth, Carl
and Gayle began to feel that they were ready to plant the church of
God's design.

Carl shares, "After prayer and discussion, we felt God would have
us plant a church in my hometown of Lincoln, Nebraska. My dad and
mom still lived in the little house where they raised my three sisters and
me. It was in their living room that we met on June 10, 1973, which
just happened to be my twenty-sixth birthday. There were five of us: a
lady who was a friend of the family, my parents, and Gayle and me."

With no financial support, the small group rented a meeting room
in the basement of an office building for twenty dollars a week. It was
the start of seeing God's vision for Calvary Community Church of
Lincoln, Nebraska, fulfilled.

Strategy

Carl committed his full attention to planting the church and spent his days knocking on doors. "I would work my way up one side of the block and back on the other. My prayer was, 'Lord, out of all these homes, help me to find one interested person.' Day after day God answered my prayer, and I would find that receptive and interested individual or family. When I did, I would write down their name and address and add them to our constantly growing mailing list."

After a summer of going door to door, the new church was ready to launch. Dr. Towns conducted the organizational service on September 24, 1973. Carl remembers the special service: "Dr. Towns spoke on the Great Commission and challenged us to build a great church. Nineteen courageous people signed on as charter members. I told them God would answer our prayers and that one day we would have a 20-acre campus with new buildings and ministries for children, teens, young adults and senior saints."

The Scripture theme for the little church became Jeremiah 32:27: "Behold, I am the LORD, the God of all flesh. Is anything too difficult for me?" The members memorized it and recited it together at every service.

At their one-year anniversary, the church reached their goal of 100 in attendance. Up until that time, Carl had received no financial support from the young church. It was time to teach the congregation to put God first in their finances. The little flock responded with great steps of faith and reached a budget goal of $500 a week. They began supporting Carl with $150 weekly and saving for the future.

Calvary Community soon outgrew the meeting room and moved to the neighborhood YMCA building.

Struggles

But even though the young church was off to a good start, Carl remembers some devastating struggles. At one point a retired minister joined the young congregation and befriended many people in the flock. As time went by, he grew critical of Carl's leadership. He left the church and influenced several other families to leave also. Carl shares "This was the first big negative setback to hit us, and it was tough to shake as we were knocked off track and lost momentum."

By Calvary Community's second anniversary, attendance was down to eighty-eight. Carl was heartbroken: "We were slipping backward, struggling to keep our flock together. This went on week by week until the weeks turned into months. People were losing the one thing a church plant must have—vision and excitement for the future."

It was during this time period that Carl's wife Gayle announced that she was praying God would give the church $25,000. It was the annual income of the church. Carl didn't see how that would happen. The excitement of the ship's launching and the maiden voyage of the first year was over. Things didn't look good. Carl was tempted to quit.

> Discouragement came over me in waves. I spent whole nights in the Y building down on my face on the mats wrestling with God in prayer. We just could not get unstuck; everything was down—attendance, giving and our spirits. The battle continued and after carrying this heavy burden for nearly a year, I finally decided, "That's it! God must not want us in Lincoln. We must have missed it when we felt called to come home." The decision was made; we will call it quits and move on. The struggle was over. I went to bed and went to sleep.

Carl may have thought the decision was made, but God had other plans.

> The next morning I went into the bathroom to shave and on a piece of paper taped to the corner of the mirror was Scripture in Gayle's handwriting. Actually, it had been there for weeks. But as I read the Scripture, it was as if I heard God's voice out of the heavens speaking to me. "But thanks be to God, who gives us the victory through our Lord Jesus Christ. Therefore, my beloved

brethren, be steadfast, immovable, always abounding in the work of the Lord, knowing that your toil is not in vain in the Lord" (1 Corinthians 15:57-58, NASB). My tears ran into my shaving cream as I said, "OK, Lord, I'll stay—even if we have to spend our lives meeting in a rented building and sitting on folding chairs."

Again, Carl showed the determination and tenacity to follow God's vision.

Successes

Not long after this, Carl heard about land for sale just outside of town. He and Gayle drove out to see the property. It was strategically located between Interstates 80 and 180, and from the crest of the property they could see the skyline of the city. Carl remembers the moment: "We found an old bale of hay that the farmer had left there. Gayle and I knelt by that bale and prayed, 'God, if You would give us this property, and if You would let us, we will spend our lives building a church here for You.'"

Carl met with the owner of the property, who was asking $5,000 an acre—$25,000 for the five acres. Carl shared the vision God had given him to spend his life in Lincoln, building a church that would reach many for Christ. Then Carl asked the owner if he would be willing to give half the property to Calvary Community, basically a contribution of $12,500. "Then I prayerfully waited what seemed like an eternity for his response," Carl writes . "My heart jumped for joy when he said, 'Yes, I'll do that.'"

Carl loaded up the little flock on a bus and took them to see the land. He told them the great news and that they needed to match the gift with $12,500. The church had a savings account of $2,000. Carl shares "Our people recognized this as an opportunity from God, and everyone rose to the occasion. We raised the $10,500 and paid the landowner the $12,500."

Afterwards, they realized that God had answered Gayle's prayer and given the church $25,000! It was the beginning of many answered prayers. Carl describes how far Calvary Community Church has come:

> God has "enlarged our borders" (1 Chronicles 4:10) and today we have at First and Superior Streets a 36-acre campus for our church and Christian school. We have a debt-free ministry and are building now for the fifth time. Our new worship center will enable us to more than double our ministry capacity to 1,500-2,000 people. And, of course, we have Elmer Towns scheduled to dedicate our new building on May 17, 2009, just as he has after the completion of each of our buildings.

Soul

The passion of Calvary Community Church is reflected in the purpose statement of the congregation: "We exist to lead people into a growing relationship with Christ. We believe a great commitment to the Great Commission (Matthew 28:19-20) and the Great Commandment (Matthew 22:37–40) will grow a great church."

Calvary Community Church is a place of love and acceptance. The services are a blend of both traditional and upbeat contemporary elements with messages designed to help people apply God's Word to their everyday lives. Calvary Community Church ministries include adult small groups, young adult groups, men and women's ministries, student ministries, and children's ministry.

Significance

Not long after opening a Christian school in 1980, Calvary Community faced a David versus Goliath challenge with the State of Nebraska.

The teachers union—with nearly 20,000 teachers—was the most powerful union in the state. And of all the states, Nebraska had the most restrictive educational laws: every school was required to apply for a state license. The licensing process included approval of curriculum and teachers. Carl says "Because our school was a ministry of our church, we felt the autonomy of the church must be protected and that we could not submit part of our church to the government."

It was a legal battle that went on for two years and took a great toll on the ministry. Carl shares that he "often reminded people that it was a privilege to stand on the front line for religious freedom in America. Religious people were attacked all across the state. The Amish sold their land and moved out of the state. Home school parents were taken to court, churches were fined, and a few pastors were jailed. We organized Nebraskans for Religious Freedom, and I was asked to serve as chairman; so I was not only a pastor, but also leading a statewide battle for freedom."

The media did its best to make Calvary Community look like unreasonable, right-wing radicals. The number of visitors to the church dwindled. There was a dark cloud over the ministry.

With the help of Dr. Jerry Falwell, Calvary Community contacted a nationally known constitutional attorney named William Ball of Harrisburg, Pennsylvania, who took the case.

The next two years of litigation cost over $100,000. As the struggle continued week by week, month after month for two years, church attendance dropped 40 percent, and the future looked bleak. During those dark days, Carl often received encouraging calls from Jerry Falwell.

And many other members of the church stood strong and firm, committed to the vision. Carl remembers,

> God's people all across America prayed for and supported us and finally we won the battle. What a glorious day that was when victory finally came. Today, many students in Nebraska are in Christian schools and home schools free of government control.

In 1995, Liberty University honored Carl with an honorary doctor's degree. Carl recalls, "When Jerry put the cape on me and gave me the degree, I thanked him for such a great honor and then turned to the crowd and pointed to Gayle. Jerry had her stand and introduced her.

As I sat down and wiped the moisture from my eyes, I thought, "God, You've sure been good to this PK (plumber's kid)."

Summary

As one of the first church planters to blossom under the influence of Dr. Jerry Falwell and Liberty University, Carl Godwin is a shining example of a godly man committed to the vision and passionate about making a difference in the lives of others.

What's the key? Carl explains it this way,

It was during the difficult days of the school battle that I began waking up at 3 or 4 a.m. and could not go back to sleep. I was under a boatload of stress. I decided I needed to exercise, so I began to run. I was a convenience runner; if my schedule allowed, if the weather was nice, I would run, therefore, I was inconsistent. Then as I got into my 50s I decided to go from a convenience runner to a committed runner. To motivate myself I registered for a 10K race. Now I have run 21 races, including 12 marathons. At 60 years of age I ran the highlight of my races, the Super Bowl of distance running, the grand daddy of them all—the Boston Marathon.

Many times I have recalled what Jerry Falwell said, "The test of a man is what it takes to discourage him." As I reflect back over 36 years of ministry, I realize that my life verse, 1 Corinthians 15:57–58 is the key. It is knowing that our victory is in Christ and remaining steadfast, unmovable and abounding in His work. As God says, "look to Jesus" and "run with endurance" (Hebrews 12:1).

Ministry is a marathon. That is why God says, "Run with endurance." I'm still running and ministering because it is not how you start, but how you finish that counts. We want to finish well and "run that we may win" (1 Corinthians 9:24).

ABOUT THE CHURCH PLANTER—

Carl Godwin is the Senior Pastor and founder of Calvary Community Church of Lincoln, Nebraska (www.mycalvary.org). The church's purpose is to lead people into a growing relationship with Jesus Christ.

Having accepted Christ as his personal Savior as a child, Carl felt God's calling to the pastorate at the age of sixteen. Following graduation from Lincoln High School, he received his B.A. and M.A. degrees from Bible college. In 1995, he was awarded an honorary doctoral degree from Liberty University.

Carl and the former Gayle Wooldridge met during college and have been married more than thirty years. They have three children and five grandchildren.

Chapter 3
It Takes Faith

"I knew that God wanted me to start a church, but I did not know where. (I told God) I am not coming down from this mountain until You show me where I should start a church."

- David Rhodenhizer

Elmer Towns, in his book, *Capturing a Town for Christ,* tells the story of a man coming to Christ and the impact his decision made on his entire family.

> Red Rhodenhizer sat in his living room as a broken man. Alcohol was beginning to destroy his life and the life of his family. It came to the point where his job was in danger. Red thought of a man with whom he worked. That man's life was different. He prayed before lunch, always seemed joyful and never got upset. He had once told Red that he had given his life to Jesus Christ and that Red should consider doing the same.

> In tears, Red at last called this friend for help. Within the hour, he and two other men came to the Rhodenhizer home, shared with Red and his wife Frances the gospel of Jesus Christ and asked if they wanted to surrender their lives to Him. On their knees by the living-room couch, they accepted Christ as their personal Savior.

> Although now in heaven, Red shared in Towns' book, "God took the thirst for alcohol away immediately."

Red wanted to grow and began attending a neighboring church, Thomas Road Baptist Church. He and his family quickly became active in the church and responded to the teaching and preaching of a young pastor named Jerry Falwell.

When Thomas Road Baptist Church decided to expand its bus ministry, Jerry gave Red the first new bus route. For the first time in his life Red had a responsibility for others, for not just their physical needs but also their spiritual needs. Red wrote, "I look back now and thank Jerry for his faith in me. I needed the responsibility for the souls of those children."

Red had been very close to his own two boys, David and Mike, and had always tried to have them in church on Sunday morning. The boys, then twelve and fourteen years old, saw a change in their parent's life. Soon the whole family began attending Thomas Road Baptist Church.

Red's son David recalls his early years, as well as his wife's, at Thomas Road Baptist Church:

Linda and I both came to Christ through the ministry of Thomas Road Baptist Church. Linda gave her heart to Christ at a Vacation Bible School when she was 12 years old. A Sunday School teacher led me to Christ at the age of 14, on August 28, 1966. When I was 16 years old, Dr. Falwell was preaching, and even though I don't recall the content of the message, God was dealing with me and I was under conviction. During the invitation, I went forward and a godly man, Mr. Mayberry, met me and took me to a counseling room to speak with me. He asked me what was wrong. I shared with him that I was saved, but I was not serving the Lord as I should. I began to weep. God was breaking me, and this would be a life-transforming event in my life.

As David left the room, he felt an overwhelming burden and desire to share his faith. He claimed the verse, Acts 1:8, "But ye shall receive power, after that the Holy Ghost is come upon you: and ye shall be witnesses unto me both in Jerusalem, and in all Judea, and in Samaria, and unto the uttermost part of the earth."

David continues his story of God moving him with a call to ministry.

In the summer of 1968 I had the opportunity to join a group of men who were evangelizing Lynchburg for Thomas Road Baptist Church. One of those men was R. C. Worley. This dear 60-year-old man of God would have a tremendous impact on my life. He was a bold witness for Christ and a man who knew how to pray. What a blessing it was to be with him and observe his life as he served Christ. I am thankful for his mentorship in my life.

He continues,

God had begun to stir my heart about full time ministry before that summer event. In May of 1968, I gave my life to the Lord to use in ministry to preach the gospel. In a way, my situation was unique because I had a speech impediment at the time. While it would be easy and natural for some to think that I was making a mistake, I can say I have never doubted my call into ministry. Looking back, what could have been considered a handicap was really a great blessing. The ministry that would take place through my life, He would have to do. Faith for me would not be, "Lord, you heal me and I will preach." Faith for me would be, "Lord, I will preach whether you heal me or not."

Elmer Towns, in his book, *Fasting Can Change Your Life*, writes about David's struggle with his calling.

At the age of 16, Dave surrendered to the Lord's call to preach, but (Jerry) Falwell was not sure of his usefulness in ministry because David stuttered. Regardless of David's inability to understand why God would call him to preach despite his speech impediment, he has never doubted the call. As David looks back on those early days of his Christian journey, he realizes now that what he may have considered as one of the worst things in his life (the speech problem) was in reality one of the best things God could ever have done for him.

David also shares about his call to the ministry with Towns and the barriers he had to overcome.

When my pastor, Dr. Jerry Falwell, heard that I had surrendered my life to preach the gospel, he thought I had somehow misread the leading of the Lord. After all, if I could not communicate reasonably well, how could I preach? When I was a junior in high school, I met with a man from the Virginia Board of Vocational Rehabilitation. During my time with him, he told me that, essentially, because of my speech impediment, I was being offered a scholarship to attend either the University of Virginia or Virginia Polytechnic Institute. Basically, all that I would need would be my parents' signatures. Looking back, I suppose those schools offered good speech therapy courses and I assumed this was the reason the offer was being made. But not long before this meeting, God had called me to preach. I had one question for this gentleman. Could they help me through a Christian school? He kindly shared with me that they could not and so my answer was very simple. God would put me through a Christian school.

Many probably would think I was making a mistake, but I knew in my heart that I was doing exactly what God had told me. Although I had difficulty speaking, I knew God would take care of my speech impediment.

My responsibility was to obey Him and to be faithful to His call.

During those early days, David had a desire to preach but couldn't find the opportunity. People were supportive, but only to a point. They really doubted whether David could stand behind a pulpit without any embarrassment.

Eventually, he was asked to speak in an adult Sunday school class for Ed Martin. David says, "I will always be grateful for his confidence in me."

David shares about future opportunities,

Next, an opportunity to teach a Sunday school class at Thomas Road Baptist Church came my way. R. C. Worley and I led the class. To this day, I'm not sure whether the class was given to me or to Brother Worley. I taught and he prayed and served as bouncer in this class of 13-year-old boys. I loved it! This growing, exciting Sunday School class was a great blessing and encouragement to me.

One of the boys in that Sunday school class was Steve Reynolds, who is currently Senior Pastor of Capitol Baptist Church in Annandale, Virginia.

Dave continues,

When I was a senior at E. C. Glass High School, the Lord impressed on me to start a Bible club in the public school. I remember going to the principal's office to seek his permission to begin the club. As we talked, he was not only pleased and supportive, but he also related to me that he had attended a Christian college. He gave me permission. Once a week on Friday I met with a few students for Bible study and prayer before classes began. This was a great step of faith as I watched God orchestrate the details. As a young man, I can remember the concern, even the hurt, of not understanding why

I would be called to preach and not be able to speak very well. Opportunities to speak and preach were slow to come my way because of my problem. People were never cruel, but, at the same time, I believe they thought they were sparing my feelings by not asking me to speak.

David attended Baptist Bible College in Springfield, Missouri, during the 1970–1971 school years. He returned home and married Linda Londeree on June 5, 1971, with Dr. Falwell and Ed Martin performing the ceremony.

Dr. Falwell was starting a new college called Lynchburg Baptist College. Linda and David enrolled and became part of that first student body in 1971. David graduated from Lynchburg Baptist College (now Liberty University) in 1974 with a B.S. degree. He was ordained on October 11, 1974.

Story

David was serving on staff at West Huntsville Baptist Church in Huntsville, Alabama, when God began to stir his heart about starting a church. In August 1977, the Rhodenhizers traveled to Lynchburg for a family vacation time. David's desire to start a church was now growing intense. He knew God wanted him to start a church but just didn't know where.

One day he drove up to Liberty Mountain and parked the car, got out, and prayed, "Lord, I'm not coming down from this mountain until you show me where You would have me to start a church." He didn't know how long he was on the mountain, but God laid on his heart the city of Alexandria, Virginia.

David shares the next series of confirming events:

I had an appointment to meet with Dr. Falwell soon after my time on the mountain. When I walked into his office he said to me, "Dave, what I would like for you to do is come back to Virginia and start a church either in Tidewater or in Northern Virginia." When he made reference to Northern Virginia, it served as a point of confirmation, yet I decided to seek further counsel. While driving to Salem, Virginia, to speak to a pastor with whom I had previously served, I received God's peace to start a church in Alexandria.

David and his family moved to Northern Virginia in September 1977. They had one prospect.

David and Linda began to meet with interested people in their home and began planning toward the first service. New Life Baptist Church held its first service on October 23, 1977. They had rented a school building and had 51 people at that first Sunday. By the end of the first year of ministry there were 64 recorded professions of faith, 51 baptisms and 108 members.

In 1979, a struggling church in Alexandria contacted David and asked if he would consider being their pastor. David again sought God's directions and determined that if this church wanted to call him as their pastor, then they would need to take all of New Life Baptist as a package.

On June 10, 1979, New Life Baptist Church merged with Calvary Road Baptist Church. On that special day, Dr. Elmer Towns presided over the marriage of the two churches.

Strategy

The Rhodenhizers focused on meeting people in their home and sharing with them the Gospel of Jesus Christ. His commitment to personal soul winning and sharing his faith developed his complete dependence on the Lord.

Successes

The merger of two churches to become Calvary Road Baptist Church provided the community with an incredible picture of what God could do. The church had about a million dollar debt, which eventually was paid in full. While paying off that debt, the church also raised the funds to build an addition to the auditorium. This required and developed great faith in the hearts and souls of the church.

David shares with Dr. Towns another account of trust and faith in God:

> My daughter Melodie had *patent ductus*, a heart defect. A specialist at Georgetown University Hospital was treating her. We were just starting the church ... there were a lot of pressures ... and one morning as I had my devotions, I read from John 15:7, "If ye abide in me, and my words abide in you, ye shall ask what ye will, and it shall be done unto you." I told the Lord that if He didn't do something special for me that day I would just as soon die. I asked the Lord to heal my little girl. We went to the hospital for the first procedure, which was a cardiac catheterization. We were briefed about what could happen. She would possibly need heart surgery, and she could have brain damage. You can't imagine what that did to my wife, Linda, and me. The doctor came back to the hospital room after the procedure, scratching his head. He said, "I just don't understand it, it's gone! It had shown up on the X-rays, but it is gone."
>
> The Lord answered prayer and healed her. That answer to prayer did something for our new church. That new church learned that God really does answer prayer.

From the ministry side of Calvary Road Baptist Church, it is one of the most progressive traditional, independent Baptist churches in the Northern Virginia area. With multiple ministries, Calvary Road supports a large Christian School, graded programs, multi-cultural and multi-ethnic ministries, and a Bible Institute.

Struggles

Personal struggles are evident in the early years of David's life as he was convinced of his call to the ministry. His confidence is seen in the faith that he developed as a young man with a difficult speech impediment. He relates,

> As a teenager, I can remember kneeling beside my bed, broken, at times even weeping, because I did not understand why God would call me to preach when I could not talk. Now, as I look back on it, what I thought was the worst thing in my life—my speech impediment—had motivated me to completely rely upon the Lord's strength and trust Him to do in my life what only He could do. I had no natural talents or abilities. Whatever God was going to do with my life, He would have to do.

Significance

David readily shares that the overall significance of Calvary Road Baptist Church is seen in reaching those who need Christ. He quotes from Eric Reamer, a former naval officer who was called into the ministry at Calvary Road, served on church staff, and left to start a church in the Albany, New York, area. Pastor Reamer shares,

> One of the main purposes of the church is to equip the saints for ministry. This has been accomplished in our lives. Oh, we are far from perfect; yet Calvary Road has been the "greenhouse" for our growth as Christians. This church and these people will provide opportunities for spiritual and personal growth for anyone who is truly open to what God has in store for them and truly willing to obey Him.

In review, one of the other major significances of Calvary Road Baptist Church and Dr. David Rhodenhizer has been the longevity of his ministry. For more than thirty years, David has built and established a landmark ministry in the suburbs of Washington, DC.

Summary

Regardless of the style of ministry that a pastor may choose, Dr. Rhodenhizer believes that "there is a discipline that a pastor must embrace as a priority every day … meet with God! It could be said that this discipline is your 'life-line.' A pastor must choose to read his Bible and pray every day." He continues,

> I would encourage pastors to realize that even though they consistently prepare messages to preach, that is not a substitute for time in the Word and in prayer. A pastor must not become so busy in the work of the Lord that he neglects his own spiritual nourishment. Jesus saved you, Jesus called you into His service, and it will be Jesus who will sustain you in day-to-day service. I believe that men of God, like Dr. Jerry Falwell, finished well, not by accident, but because of this discipline of meeting with the Lord every day.

Soul

The soul of Calvary Road Baptist Church is their passion and commitment to winning people to Christ. In every area of ministry the purpose is the same. Win them!

Statistics and Structure

Calvary Road Baptist Church is a Pastor-led church. It is served by a board of deacons. There are currently 1,500 in attendance with a pastoral staff of sixteen. They have had a high attendance of over 2,000 people. More than thirty people have been called into full-time ministry. The campus of Calvary Road Baptist houses facilities for a Christian School, Bible Institute, and expanding ministries of the church.

ABOUT THE CHURCH PLANTER—

David M. Rhodenhizer is founding and Senior Pastor of Calvary Road Baptist Church (www.crbc.org), an independent Baptist church in Alexandria, Virginia. The purpose of Calvary Road is to instruct in

God's Word to produce maturity, be involved in ministry using spiritual gifts, fellowship with other believers, and evangelize to reach the lost.

David and his wife Linda grew up in Lynchburg, Virginia, and have served together in ministry since 1971.

Pastor Rhodenhizer is a 1974 graduate of Lynchburg Baptist College (Liberty University) in Lynchburg, VA (B.S., Pastoral Ministries) and received an honorary Doctorate of Divinity degree in 1985. He was ordained at Thomas Road Baptist Church in Lynchburg, Virginia, in 1974.

He is the author of *One Like Spirit ... One Great Vision: A Journey of Faith*. David also serves on the Liberty University Board of Trustees.

David and Linda were high school sweethearts, and both began their relationship with God as teenagers. They were married in 1971 and have five children: Chris (1973), Jason (1975), Melodie (1976), Jeremy (1979), and Holly (1981), as well as twelve grandchildren.

Chapter 4
Re-Planting a Church Plant

"Holy fire, burn away my desire for anything that is not of You and is of me. I want more of You and less of me. Empty me, empty me ... fill, won't You fill me with You, with You.

"Won't You empty me now ... I want more of You, Jesus!"

- John Comer and Gene Way

Story

If you ask Danny Hodges why his church is successful, he will tell you, "It's all God ... I've been along for the ride." If you ask him what he has done to build this church, he will tell you, "Nothing, except stay out of God's way. I'm as inadequate to pastor and lead this church today as I was the first day when they handed me the keys."

Yet Calvary Chapel of St. Petersburg is a testament to what God can do with someone who is completely yielded to Him. This church, on the Gulf coast of Florida, has a weekly attendance of 4,000 in three services. It meets in a renovated Wal-Mart that the church purchased several years ago. When you walk into the large main foyer of the church, you are greeted with a warm and inviting welcome area. In the very middle is a play area for children outfitted with toys to develop motor skills and awareness. In the rear right corner, the area that used to be a McDonalds restaurant is now a full service café offering everything from breakfast to weekly dinner specials. To the left of the café is a coffee area where those in attendance are able to talk and share a cup. To the far left of the foyer is a Missions Café that serves a light fare with all proceeds going to missions projects for the church. Just to the left of the Missions Café is a full-scale bookstore carrying Bibles, resource material, and the latest messages and teachings of the church pastors and staff.

As you leave the foyer and proceed to the auditorium, you pass by one of the most inviting children's areas around. Walls are decorated with life-size characters and wall writings of verses that would tickle the imagination of any child.

There are two places of worship: the worship center, which holds almost 1,200, and a family worship area where parents can sit together with young children and worship.

The worship is passionate and full. The messages are challenging and authentic. The invitations are life-changing. There is no offering taken during the service: worshippers are encouraged to give their tithes and gifts as they leave the service in designated locations.

During the services there are shuttles that run to several remote locations bringing people to the front door. There is a safety ministry that roams the facility during each service to provide assistance and security whenever needed. There are other ministries taking place and being promoted throughout the church, and hundreds of volunteers share in the work of the ministry.

When you ask Senior Pastor Danny Hodges how each of these ministries began, he will tell you, using a basketball analogy that he "likes to pass the ball." The ministries are not all because of him; they are a result of saints feeling the call of God to step up and be involved. He passed the ball, and they ran with it.

Did Danny grow up in a ministry home? Was he prepared to lead this great church by following the examples of others growing up? Far from it.

Like too many, Danny came from a broken home. His mother was divorced when he was four years old and then remarried a short time later. By the time he reached fourth grade, his step-father adopted both him and his older brother. Danny went from being Danny Griggs to Danny Hodges in one day. Whenever such a change happens, the results are unknown.

Soon after, he began to rebel and live life independently of his mother, grandmother, or any other figure who became an authority in his life. By middle school he was experimenting with marijuana and before long was trying just about any drug that came along. Near the end of his junior year of high school he was expelled from school as a result of drug use and addiction.

Danny spent the next couple of years searching for something in life that would finally satisfy his emptiness and need to belong. No amount of drugs, parties, or girlfriends worked. He had a hole inside that nothing could fill.

Deep down he knew what he needed. He had learned about Jesus Christ through his mother and grandmother, but had never received Christ as Savior. For months, he thought about yielding his life but kept resisting.

One evening he came home from a local bar. It was a weeknight in a small town in South Carolina, so there wasn't much activity. His mother and grandmother were watching a prime time television special with a preacher named Jack Van Impe. Danny didn't want them to know he was listening, so he hid around the corner in the kitchen. When the preacher gave the invitation to receive Christ, God got a hold of Danny's heart.

He went out into the front yard, knelt before God, and gave his life to Christ. That was the beginning of a journey that would provide significance to a young man who had struggled with knowing who he was and whose he was.

As a new believer, Danny needed to grow in his faith. On a Sunday evening, he responded to an altar call surrendering for full-time service in the ministry. His counselor had attended Liberty University and recommended that Danny look at that school. Not knowing how he would pay for school, Danny enrolled and attended by faith, trusting God for what He was going to do.

God provided, often through Danny working two to three jobs, and led Danny to become part of ministry group called Youth Aflame. Danny had a desire to work with young people and to teach them the Word of God, sharing the power of what God could do in their lives, just as He had in Danny's life.

During his years at Liberty, Danny was impressed with the determination and faith of Dr. Falwell. He saw devotion, dedication, and dependence on God through the walk of Dr. Falwell that would influence him in his ministry life.

Under the ministry of Youth Aflame, Danny was able to take the truth he had learned in the classroom and apply it in weekend ministry opportunities. Having a love for music, he played the drums and helped with setup for the musical programs.

It was during these long and exhausting weekends that God began to give Danny a vision for reaching out to others with the gospel of Christ. Young people were hurting—yet they were also hungry to find a solution for the pain and hurt in their lives. Danny had experienced that same hurt and pain, and he knew the answer was found in Christ.

On these ministry trips, God also challenged Danny by introducing him to people who did not share his denominational roots, yet still had a passion and love for God that often exceeded Danny's. He began to see that the body of Christ was far more diverse and broad than he had ever understood.

In August 1982, some of Danny's friends in St. Petersburg, Florida, gathered a small group of believers together in an apartment with a young single pastor to form a new church. This group gradually grew and called themselves "Calvary Chapel." The pastor and a few others in the church had attended Liberty Baptist College (now Liberty University) in Virginia. Danny had graduated with a degree in Youth Ministry in the spring of 1982, and when he came down for a visit to play drums in a concert sponsored by this newly formed church he was asked to consider joining the church to work with junior high students.[11]

---

11   Calvary Chapel Church History: A Look Back At Our Beginnings, [need further info]

Confident that God had called him into full-time Christian work—perhaps with youth—Danny sought the Lord's direction for full-time ministry. He had prayed about several opportunities and was eager to gain the experience of working in a ministry from the ground up. Though he was still unsure of a specific calling, he felt a confirmation to take part in the young church that had only been meeting for one year.

In August of 1983, Danny moved from Virginia to St. Petersburg, Florida, with dreams of starting a junior high ministry in Calvary Chapel. Several months later, through an unexpected turn of events, the pastor was led to return to the hometown, and other church leadership needed to focus on areas of ministry outside of Calvary Chapel.

The decision was made to close the church doors and accept that Calvary Chapel would no longer be in existence as a local fellowship in the St. Petersburg area. Danny was certain that he had sensed the leadership of God in moving to this new church, and his spirit was not comfortable in closing down the church. He recalls the meeting and his comment to those in leadership, "I don't feel that God wants us to close the doors of this church." Danny had asked the church leadership to hold off on the decision and give him the opportunity pray and seek God's direction. This would become one of many times that Danny would go before God and pour his heart out seeking God's face and leadership.

His heart remembered God's confirmation on his coming to this church. He recalled the many times Dr. Falwell talked about not quitting and never giving up. He remembered the many lessons—taught and caught—about making decisions based on faith and not sight.

Danny went back and met with this young church leadership team and said that he was confident that "God did not want to close this church." With that, the pastor handed him the keys to the building and said it was his to lead. Danny states, "I never felt such a sense of inadequacy as when they handed me the keys to the church and said it's yours. I had no idea what God wanted to do."

Danny was asked to become the pastor of this small group that wanted to continue meeting together. After much more prayer and consideration, and believing this to be that specific call of God, Danny accepted the position and became the new pastor of Calvary Chapel in April 1984.

Strategy

Danny recalls the early years of Calvary Chapel, "We initially met in 'The Sons of Italy' Lodge. Each weekend we would take down the beer signs from the walls and have church. As soon as church was over, we would put them back up. This was part of the routine each week."

Over the next few years, through his own personal study of Scripture, Pastor Danny felt personally challenged in three specific areas.

First, he believed the Bible clearly taught that all spiritual gifts are available to believers today, just as they were in the early church, but that they should be exercised appropriately according to scriptural guidelines. Pastor Danny felt a sincere desire to teach through the Word of God and avoid extremism, particularly concerning areas often left to private interpretation.[12]

Second was the area of praise and worship. Not only was he personally challenged to truly worship the Lord "in spirit and in truth," but he sought to have a church service where believers could openly and freely express their praise and worship to God in a heartfelt way that was real and uncontrived. While he appreciated traditional hymns, he enjoyed the more contemporary praise music and longed to one day have a praise band that would inspire and facilitate genuine worship.[13]

Third was his desire to be "real" and to have a fellowship of believers whose faith in Christ was real, not phony, plastic, or simply religious. As a result, his style of dress for church serviced gradually became more casual, as he wanted those who attended, especially unbelievers, to feel comfortable just as they were, without feeling it was necessary to get dressed up. He wanted all to feel equally welcome and accepted, from

---

12   Ibid
13   Ibid

the homeless to wealthy professionals, and to understand that dress does not determine godliness.[14]

Kim Correy is married to Bob, Pastor of Worship at Calvary Chapel. Kim has been at Calvary Chapel since day one. If you ask her about the growth of Calvary, she will say that "It's Christian Real". The church reflects the pastor. She describes Pastor Danny as "being humble." She says, "He teaches what he himself needs. He includes himself in the lesson."

David Morrin is a shuttle bus driver who has attended Calvary for the past few years. He shares that "Pastor Danny is real and he can relate to those who have really struggled in life ... those who have lost hope." He says, "It's simple. It's praise and worship, life-changing teaching and dependent prayer."

Pastor Danny says "our strategy has always been Acts 2:42: 'They were continually devoting themselves to the apostles' teaching and to fellowship, to the breaking of bread and to prayer'" (NASB).

With this approach to ministry, Pastor Danny began to feel somewhat out of place among other churches. Although he enjoyed fellowship with other local pastors, he wasn't sure who he could identify with in terms of his style of ministry. He was seeking a balance between the extremes of Pentecostalism and Fundamentalism without compromising the Word of God.[15]

Three years later, as a result of numerous visitors from other churches called Calvary Chapel, Pastor Danny attended a pastor's conference in Costa Mesa, California, and was introduced to Pastor Chuck Smith and the Calvary Chapel movement. Danny felt immediately at home and grateful that God had led him to this fellowship of churches that upheld a simple, biblical philosophy of ministry and a well-balanced doctrine. Calvary Chapel St. Petersburg became a fellowship of Calvary Chapel Costa Mesa.[16]

---

14   Ibid
15   Ibid
16   www.ccstpete.com, Our History

As Pastor Danny looks toward the coming year of ministry, he has felt impressed to claim four principles of ministry:

1. Proverbs 27:23 (NASB): *"Know well the condition of your flocks, and pay attention to your herds."* Pastor Danny openly admits that Calvary has grown more than he ever thought possible. He also admits that as one pastor, he is not able to know the condition of each member of his flock. His prayer for upcoming ministry is that God will raise up new ministry leaders who will share in the shepherding of the flock. As has been the strategy of Calvary Chapels, most staff members come from within the congregation: they are ministry leaders who have been faithful and fruitful in their ministry. Leadership development is a key strategy for the future of Calvary Chapel.

2. Acts 3:7 (NASB): *"And seizing him by the right hand, he raised him up, and immediately his feet and his ankles were strengthened."* Peter and John had gone to the temple during the ninth hour, the hour of prayer. A man who had been lame since birth and who had been carried to the gate Beautiful asked them for alms. Pastor Danny makes the point that this lame man had probably been at the temple during the ministry of Jesus, yet had not been healed. As Peter reached out, the man was immediately healed. Pastor Danny feels Calvary Chapel will be reaching out to people who have been previously ignored. Reaching those who have not been reached is another key strategy for Calvary Chapel in the future.

3. Acts 5:28 (NASB): *"We gave you strict orders not to continue teaching in this name, and yet, you have filled Jerusalem with your teaching."*. Pastor Danny has sensed that Calvary Chapel must continue to "saturate" the Tampa Bay area with the Gospel of Jesus Christ, using technology, the Internet, and whatever means God provides to reach the greatest number of people with the best possible means. This concept of "saturation evangelism" is rooted in the ministry strategy of Dr. Falwell and Thomas Road Baptist Church. Saturating the community with the Gospel of Christ is a key strategy for Calvary Chapel.

4. Romans 13:8 (NASB): *"Owe nothing to anyone except to love one another."* Pastor Danny has sensed from God that the next phase of Calvary Chapel's ministry is to eliminate the burden of

debt from the church and from those within the congregation. Following God's principles for finance and giving will be a key strategy for Calvary Chapel.

Successes

When asked about the successes of Calvary Chapel, Pastor Danny's response is very concise. When asked about what God has done, he is equally exact in the source of the success of this sun coast church. Regarding God's role in doing what only He could do, Pastor Danny says, "Everything! Only God could take a guy like me and pull off this kind of ministry."

He continues, "People are saved pretty much every week. Our outreach continues to increase, and we have a great staff." Kim Correy commented that one of the successes of Calvary Chapel is that they predominantly hire from within. As people come to church and begin to grow, they usually get involved in ministry. Those who develop a commitment to the work, those who develop a heart for helping others, and those who are seen as "servant-leaders" are the first ones considered when staffing needs arise.

Kim comments, "Doesn't that make the most sense? We have grown from nothing to this huge church. Only someone who has experienced this can have a proper perspective as to how we do ministry."

Hiring from within also credits the priority of developing lay leadership with the body. Pastor Danny often says, "Healthy sheep reproduce other healthy sheep." The health of the congregation begins with a steady diet of God's teaching on the basis of Scripture and the benefits of a changed heart. Danny's commitment to study and teaching have been a strong factor in the success of Calvary Chapel.

Leadership development and growth are also vital to the creation, development and implantation of ministries within the body of the church. Of the multifaceted ministries that are practiced every week, many have been birthed in the hearts of believers. They have sensed God's leading, have gone to Pastor Danny, and have asked about developing a new ministry. After prayer and commitment to God's leadership, Danny often "passes them the ball" and provides them the support, encouragement, and resources to "charge" with the ministry that God has laid on their heart. Danny says, "If they own it, they will grow it." This encourages believers to be involved in the "work of the ministry" and the "building up of the body of Christ."

From the youngest children's ministries to Golgotha Skate Park to almost fifty home-based fellowship gatherings in multiple cities called LIFEgroups to various Women's ministries to multiple Men's ministries to fully graded programs—each ministry has a distinct purpose to grow the individual into a vibrant life as a follower of Christ Jesus.

One of the other key success factors of Calvary Chapel is the systematic, practical, and insightful teaching that occurs every week from the pulpit. Pastor Danny places a priority on the study of God's Word. The intense study of Scripture confirmed Danny's calling and role as pastor of Calvary Chapel. He also credits the regular teaching of God's Word for the growth of those he shepherds.

"We don't just teach from the Bible. We teach through the Bible. We start at Genesis, and we don't stop until we get to Revelation. We do it verse by verse. Then we start over again," says Hodges.

A young member of the church, Jody, shares, "I love Calvary Chapel because we live by the Word of God. We are not afraid to teach the truth and share the Gospel of Jesus Christ."

The work of grace in the lives of members of Calvary Chapel has been captured in a book entitled *Stories of Calvary*, written by Mary Fairchild and Pastor Danny.

Stories of Calvary is a collection of twenty stories told by real people. It is a testament to God's incredible power to transform lives. The common strand woven through each one speaks of amazing change that begins at the cross of Calvary, when ordinary men and women encounter an extraordinary Savior, Jesus Christ.

Stories are told of lives being transformed at Calvary Chapel. Hopes are restored, dreams are renewed, and fears are overcome. Alcoholics, drug dealers, and prescription drug addicts are truly set free. A lesbian woman, a gay man, an unwed mother, a convicted felon, and a woman tormented with pain have their lives changed in miraculous ways. These are stories of promise and assurance.[17]

Struggles

Danny is open in sharing the major struggle he faces: "feeling so inadequate for the task." He is the one most surprised at what God has done through Calvary Chapel.

Hodges has often said, "Ministry is from us; it's not for us, and it's not about us."

"We really expect the Lord to be honored in more changed lives," Danny said when Calvary moved into their present location. "Because that's really what it's all about. It's not the building. It's about the people that will gather in this building to worship the Lord."

This sense has increased with the growth of the church. Danny says, "Our major challenges are the spiritual casualties in the church." Having been a broken man, he understands the testing that is required to consistently gain spiritual victory.

Significance

The significance of Calvary Chapel is seen in several areas. One has been the longevity and tenure of its Senior Pastor, Danny Hodges. Educated as a youth pastor and a confessed musician who is as surprised as anybody that God would use him, Pastor Danny has accepted his fears of being inadequate for the task and embraced the calling of this life.

His acceptance of anyone who loves Christ and who has a need has left a significant impact on his community.

This significance was seen when Hurricane Frances visited the Gulf Coast several years ago. Waveney Ann Moore of the *St. Petersburg Times* wrote this account in September 2004:

---

17   *Stories of Calvary*, Fairchild and Hodges, Winepress Publishers, Intro.

Less than a week after moving into a renovated Wal-Mart store, Calvary Chapel St. Petersburg sent word to fellow believers along Florida's east coast that it would welcome anyone fleeing the fury of Hurricane Frances.

The congregation of more than 3,000 had just finished transforming the former discount store, at 8900 U.S. 19 N, into an all-encompassing network of classrooms, offices, nurseries, youth rooms, worship space, bookstore and lobby featuring a cafe and grill.

And as Hurricane Frances bore down on Florida, church officials recognized that the 148,000-square-foot building would make an excellent refuge. After all, its walls practically constitute a fortification.

Although Calvary welcomed evacuees, it didn't need to use the church itself in the end. Instead, dozens of worshipers opened their own homes to East Coast families.[18]

Summary

In summarizing the work that God continues to do at Calvary Chapel, Danny lists three challenges to those who will plant, pastor, and shepherd churches. First, Hodges encourages pastors to devote themselves to the Lord. This devotion is seen in a regular and aggressive commitment to be a follower of Jesus and a student of His Word. Danny cannot express enough the importance of spending committed time in the Word, sacrificial time in prayer, and devoted time fasting.

Second, Danny urges young pastors to dedicate themselves to their calling as examples and shepherds of their flock. The character qualities seen in First Timothy and Titus are minimal requirements for those in ministry service. God mandates that those who are shepherds do so willingly, by example and with their whole hearts (1 Peter 5).

---

18   "Church in Wal-mart opens to evacuees," St. Petersburg Times Online, Waveney Ann Moore, September 5, 2004

Finally, Hodges recommends that pastors and church planters depend on God's anointing and not their own ability. Many pastors are great communicators and great counselors—yet these skills don't necessarily facilitate the unexplainable moving of God through the powerful teaching of His Word.

Danny remembers the life and practice of Dr. Falwell on the themes of knowing God and building His church. Although brilliant, Falwell, like Hodges. simply had an undergraduate degree from a small school, yet God was able to entrust Dr. Falwell with amazing opportunities that were activated by great faith and trust in God's provision. Hodges reminds us, "God used unschooled and ordinary men like me that simply had been with Jesus."

Soul

When asked about the passion and heartbeat of the church, Danny quickly places his explanation on Acts 2:42, "They were continually devoting themselves to the apostles' teaching and to fellowship, to the breaking of bread and to prayer."

As Danny has embraced the principles in this passage, he has seen his role and developed his passion as a teacher of the Word. His genuine sense of realness, disarming transparency, and humorous down-to-earth style has become the trademark of this expository teacher.

Statistics and Structure

In June 1997 the church moved into a 42,000-square-foot quarters that it leased in the Mainlands shopping center at 9021 U.S. 19 N. Four years later, it had outgrown the space. Over the years, the church also has spawned other congregations in Oldsmar, Madeira Beach, Ocala, and Wesley Chapel.

The current but temporary auditorium of Calvary Chapel holds 1,150 people. They have three services (one on Saturday evening, and two on Sunday morning) with each service being full in attendance. Including 600 to 800 children, Calvary Chapel averages approximately 3,800 each week. They are located on 14 acres in Pinellas County on the Gulf coast of Florida and occupy a 148,000-square-foot original Wal-Mart store.

Neither Hodges nor Calvary Chapel ever received any support from a sending church.

In 1987 Danny was led to join the fellowship of Calvary Chapels (a non-denominational movement founded by Pastor Chuck Smith of Costa Mesa, California, in the late '60s) where he found common ground among pastors who upheld the same convictions.

Calvary Chapel has 64 paid staff and hundreds of volunteers who assist with the ministry.

Calvary Chapel is a nondenominational church that is led by a senior pastor and a team of "shepherding elders." The elders assist paid staff in the spiritual oversight of the church.

Hodges points out, "We have a church board that handle all financial issues, as well as those physical plant issues that need to be addressed on a regular basis."

Regarding the type of church teaching, Danny teaches systemically through the Scriptures. He is on his third time through.

> *"I have never sat around in a meeting and tried to figure out how to get people in the church. We worship. We teach the word of God. We fellowship as believers and we pray."*
>
> *- Pastor Danny Hodges*

ABOUT THE CHURCH PLANTER—

Danny Hodges is the Senior Pastor of Calvary Chapel of St. Petersburg (www.ccstpete.com), a nondenominational church that has been formed as a fellowship of believers in the Lordship of Jesus Christ. Their supreme desire is to know Christ and be conformed to His image by the power of the Holy Spirit. Calvary Chapel St. Petersburg is a fellowship church of Calvary Chapel Costa Mesa, California, pastored by Chuck Smith.

Danny is a well-recognized Bible teacher and has published several studies and message series.

Pastor Hodges is a graduate of Liberty University in Lynchburg, VA (B.S., Youth Ministry) and was ordained as pastor of Calvary Chapel of St. Petersburg in 1983.

Married since 1986, Danny and Wendy have four children—Austin "Tanner," Hayden, Jairus, and Audra.

Chapter 5
New Hope for the Inner City

"As goes the city, so goes the nation and ultimately the world."

- Dr. Francis Schaeffer

Story

Andy Zivojinovic knew from the time he was a sophomore at Liberty University that God was calling him into ministry. But he told me his "biggest encouragement and motivation came from the life and example of Dr. Jerry Falwell."

Andy said he had always thought of pastors as "lazy" and "weak." "But Dr. Falwell's life totally changed my attitude and view of pastors," he said. Andy's idea of what it means to be a pastor would be even further challenged before God was done. God planted a passion within Andy for inner city ministry a couple years later when the late pastor and theologian Dr. Francis Schaeffer spoke in chapel at Liberty. Andy remembers it this way:

> I sat at the back of chapel so I could be one of the first ones out once the final prayer was prayed. But one statement made by Dr. Schaeffer was used by God to change the course and direction of my life. Dr. Schaeffer said, "As goes the city, so goes the nation and ultimately the world."
>
> The influence of the masses in the urban centers of America determine the direction and spirit of our nation. I believe that is because good Bible believing

churches have abandoned the masses of people in the inner city. (This) statement was the very thing that God used to grip my heart to go to the place that most Christian church planters have avoided and neglected.

During college Andy spent many summers on urban mission trips. He said, "God really gave me a love and desire for minorities and their experience."

Andy knew God was taking him to the inner city, and he wanted to be in a place where God's love could shine the brightest in the most spiritually dark areas. He chose Chicago. So in June of 1989, New Hope Bible Church began in a two-bedroom apartment on the north side of Chicago with a core of three people. Andy had been praying and reading the Bible about where to locate the church. One day while reading the book of Joshua, Andy read where God told Joshua "to go south to Kadesh Barnea." He remembers,

We had been trying for months to find a location to start the church. We had outlined a target area to focus on. After reading in Joshua, the words 'go south' just illuminated in my heart. So I prayed and asked the Lord if I should look for a building south of the southern border we had established. And I sensed that we should. After months of looking for a building, on the day I went south God gave us a building. It was not until about one year later that I found out we were in Humboldt Park, one of the worst neighborhoods in the U.S.

The Humboldt Park region was predominantly Latino and Black. It was a gang-infested community filled with drugs, violence, prostitution, poverty, brokenness, and despair. It is there that New Hope Bible Church found a home.

But the ethnic makeup of the community dictated that Andy make some radical changes to reach the community. He said, "We had to radically change the way we do church and how we do church if we were going to reach people in the inner city. We realized that if we were going to do what God wanted, we would have to be intentional about racial reconciliation and reaching people."

When it was time to launch, Andy and volunteers went door-to-door inviting people to the new church. They also passed out thousands of flyers and brochures.

Strategy

According to Andy, the New Hope Bible Church strategy is driven by seven specific God-given passions. All the programs and outreaches of the church stem from a passionate devotion to:

- racial reconciliation,

- caring for the poor, needy and homeless,

- reaching out to the thousands of gang members in the city,

- teaching sound doctrine from God's Word,

- training up indigenous minority leaders from the inner city,

- planting urban churches here and abroad, and

- training suburban churches on how to reach people cross-culturally.

The church focuses on these goals through ministries like StreetHope. It is a homeless ministry that reaches about 200 people weekly. The outreach provides food, clothing, counseling and other support to help the less fortunate get on their feet. Church staff and members have also worked with over 1,000 hard-core gang members over the years; many have come to Christ and become active members of the church. Andy said, "We have even done 50 to 100 gang-related funerals as a ministry to share God's love with them."

The church also has a dynamic youth ministry. And through the "Hope for the Hood" outreach, thousands of young people from around the country have experienced inner city ministry. Each summer hundreds of young people from across the U.S. gather at New Hope for this weeklong training and outreach ministry. The youth work in the worst areas of the city to show God's love. "They leave forever changed," Andy said. "We have hosted and trained about 18,000 young people over the past twenty years of ministry."

KidsHope reaches out to children in the streets and in the community. Another important tool of the church is a women's ministry that helps broken and battered women in the city. And the men's ministry is also a critical spiritual tool. Andy said,

> We have seen some of the hardest core people in the city come to Christ. We have led to Christ an ex–Mafia hit man who loves God and is like another apostle Paul. We have worked with and reached out to many prostitutes, lesbians, homosexuals, and transvestites in the past to let them see the love of Christ.

The church body at New Hope is diverse with about fifteen different nationalities represented. All but two of the approximately twenty ministry leaders—pastors, elders, deacons, and heads of ministry—are minority.

In addition, the church launched a college-level Bible institute to train men and women who desire to know sound doctrine from God's Word, but who do not have the funds to go to a Christian college or Bible school.

New Hope also planted another church in Richmond, Virginia. And the church has helped to plant, support, and train forty pastors and churches in Hyderabad, India. For the past seven years, New Hope has sent a couple to India for six months at a time to train and equip pastors. To continue that discipleship, New Hope plans to establish a New Hope Bible Institute at the mother church in India to provide even further theological training for the pastors there.

Andy said,

> These are things that only God can do because we are a small, poor inner city church of approximately 200

people. We draw thousands of people to our outreaches, and most people can't believe it. But what I tell people is this: "It is not how big your church is. It is how big your heart is that determines how big the ministry that you do."

Struggles

Andy admits that because of the location and calling of the church, they struggle more than most. He said,

> We lack a lot of gifted people in various areas that could really help us to greater ministry. We lack the musicians and singers that most churches have. We lack a lot of the administrative and organizational skills that others have. We greatly lack the finances to do what we know God has called us to do. We have had more failures than successes. But we see the hand of God in our church and the ministry that we do for the needy. We have hundreds saved each year through all of the different outreaches.

Andy said they need mature believers who can do the discipleship and training. They have also outgrown their current facility and struggle with a lack of finances and personnel. "But we see the cup as half full, not half empty. So we continue to persevere."

Significance

God has done some amazing things over the past 20 years at New Hope.

The church's mission is "To transform our community into spiritually mature, radically devoted followers of Christ, of all nationalities, who are willing to serve God and die for His Cause." And the mission drives every program and outreach of the church.

Andy said, "Our mission is very real to us. We truly believe it is the heart of God." Below are some distinctive characteristics of the church that make it unique.

Christ-Centered

New Hope is a Christ-honoring, Bible-centered church that does not change its theology with the shifting sands of culture. Yet church leaders incorporate culturally relevant methods of communicating the Gospel.

Community-Focused

The entire congregation is actively involved in meeting both the spiritual and physical needs of people through community outreach ministries. They also provide food, clothes, and counseling for those in need. Each believer is expected to use his or her spiritual gifts, talents, and abilities to reach people in the community for Christ. The majority of ministry takes place *outside* of the four walls of the church *in* the community.

Contemporary Service

New Hope is culturally relevant and racially sensitive to the needs of the community. The music is upbeat and lively and relates to people. Leadership works to use various modern approaches to present the living Christ to a spiritually lost world.

Cell-Based Small Groups

New Hope uses small groups for biblical fellowship, intimacy, accountability and discipleship. In the small group context, people are encouraged and instructed by applying God's Word to their daily experiences.

Culturally-Diverse

New Hope is a multiracial church that treats all people as equals. Most of the church leaders are from the community. People are dealt with on the content of their character, and not the color of their skin or race. People of all races and colors are accepted at New Hope.

Commission-Driven

New Hope members are motivated by love for God and a genuine love for people of all races. The church follows the mandate of the Great Commission and Great Commandment to make disciples of all nations (Matthew 22:37–39; 28:19–20).

Statistics

Attendance can reach as high as 325 people with about 50 to 60 youth and 30 or more children. New Hope is a multiracial church that includes about fifteen different nationalities. About 200 homeless and needy people attend the Saturday service and receive food and clothing afterwards.

About fifteen people are enrolled in the three-year Bible Institute. And about fifteen young people participate in a program of peer leadership training and equipping. One student from the church attends Liberty University, and two more expect to attend in the fall.

New Hope's first community outreach drew about 1,300 people, and the second, about 2,300 people. All of them heard the Gospel of God's love.

Support

Four other congregations have supported New Hope in the last twenty years. But most of the financial support comes from friends and individuals who share a passion for inner city ministry.

Except for Andy and his wife, New Hope's pastors and secretaries all receive their full salary from the church. Pastor Andy explains his heart:

> My wife and I receive a housing allowance from the church, and the rest of our salary we have raised like missionaries over the past twenty years. We have chosen to let the church pay the full salaries of the other pastors and staff, while we have chosen not to be a burden to the church God allowed us to birth. We have no

support from any denomination or other organization. And the church provides for all of the outreach and evangelism that we do.

Structure

New Hope is an elder-led church with Pastor Andy as the head elder. Each elder has the right to question and challenge the outreaches and ministry of the church. Andy said this structure allows the church to raise up mission-driven leaders out of the congregation. "I want men around me who are biblical thinkers, who can also at times challenge me biblically and at the same time help to sharpen me spiritually."

Worship includes theologically sound Gospel, Spanish, and Praise and Worship styles. Messages and teaching keep the Word of God simple and easy to understand without sacrificing any spiritual depth or meatiness. New Hope Bible Church is passionate about evangelism, small group ministry, discipleship, and sound doctrine. Every ministry of the church revolves around the mission statement.

Soul

The heartbeat of New Hope Bible Church is to "reach the lost at any cost." The heart and soul of the church is the desire to care for and reach out to the poor and needy, to be an agent of racial reconciliation, and to share biblically sound doctrine and theology. The stated mission is "to transform our community *into* spiritually mature, *radically devoted* followers of Christ, of *all nationalities*, who are *willing* to *serve* God and *die* for His cause" (emphasis added).

Andy said,

Everything we do flows from this mission. If you understood our community, you would understand why this mission statement is so real to us. In our community, if you are going to be radically devoted to Christ and willing to take the Gospel to the streets of the ghetto, you just may lose your life in the process. It is totally Satan's territory. That is why almost 90 percent of the churches that are planted are not in the inner city ghettos. People fear for their lives, so they don't come. They are unwilling to pay a price to reach some of society's worst and hardest people.

Go to the deserts of the inner city. We are losing our country to the liberals and socialists because most of the population of America is in the urban centers. and churches and church planters are not too excited about going there. Francis Schaeffer was correct, "As goes the city, so goes the nation."

ABOUT THE CHURCH PLANTER—

Andy Zivojinovic is the founding Pastor and head elder of the New Hope Bible Church in Chicago, Illinois, (www.newhopebiblechurch. com).

Andy is a 1984 graduate of Liberty University in Lynchburg, Virginia (B.S., Pastoral Studies). He also has a Masters of Divinity (1988). He was ordained at New Hope Bible Church in Chicago on June 5, 1994.

Andy and his wife Valerie were married on June 13, 1985. They have two sons, Josiah and Micah.

Chapter 6
Following God's Lead

"Find out where God is working and join Him."

-    Dr. Henry Blackaby, *Experiencing God*

Story

Chris Williamson knows his unique journey to become a church planter was led by God every step of the way. Born in Baltimore, Maryland, in 1968, Chris was the last of five children. At fifteen, he was saved during a citywide Christian camp. And a few years later, after visiting Liberty University, Chris and his family felt it was the place he should be.

But when he enrolled in Liberty in 1986 as a walk-on football player, it would prove to be a rocky start. Chris remembers,

> Two weeks into summer practice I broke my ankle and had to have surgery. I began school on crutches, very disillusioned and angry. I had no money for school, so I took out a student loan. One of the school's vice presidents, Michael Faulkner, took me under his wing and began to disciple me.
>
> Mr. Faulkner knew that I loved rap music, so he challenged me to write rap songs about Jesus. He took me with him when he preached and let me rap. He took me to street corners, basketball courts, detention centers and to New York City where I rapped on a subway train.

I began to see the amazing power of the gospel. That summer I traveled to three cities, New York, Philadelphia, and Chicago, doing rap evangelism with other Liberty University students.

While in New York City I led my first person to the Lord. It was at this first stop in my three-city tour that I answered the call from the Lord to preach His Word on July 4, 1987.

For his sophomore year, Chris declared Biblical Studies as his major. During that year, he also developed a relationship with his future wife, Dorena McFarland. Chris said her father, the Rev. Allen McFarland, a LBTS graduate and pastor, would become his spiritual father. One of Chris's roommates was named Daryl Fitzgerald. They grew close and began rapping together.

The two enthusiastic students soon formed a group with two other students—Andre Sims and Dillard Douglas—called Transformation Crusade. Transformation Crusade mixed rap with preaching and testimonies. Chris shares,

The four of us felt God calling us to minister in the urban centers of the United States. We had some friends on the campus who were just starting to rap and sing, too, named DC Talk. Transformation Crusade made a record and began to minister up and down the East Coast. During the summer of 1988 we traveled to thirteen cities in a Ford Thunderbird, preaching the gospel and seeing souls saved by the hundreds.

The story of one of those young people who found Christ would stay with Chris for the rest of his life. It was a boy named Tony Russell. When Tony returned home after a Transformation Crusade concert, he was gunned down as he got off the bus—a victim of gang warfare. Chris recalls,

But we knew Tony made a profession of faith in Jesus because he had signed a follow-up card that night. We were able to rejoice in that sorrowful moment.

That fall, Dr. Jerry Falwell invited the group to his office and asked them to rap at Thomas Road Baptist Church. Dr. Falwell told the students he felt blessed that they were out on the front lines, seeing souls saved. In that meeting, Dr. Falwell showed how far he was willing to go to support God's work. When he asked the students if he could do anything for them, Chris shares this exchange:

> Daryl spoke up immediately and said, "Yes. Can you pay my school bill?" Dr. Falwell replied, "Yes, I'll pay all of your school bills for as long as you want to attend Liberty University." So from my junior year through seminary I was blessed to have "JFS" (Jerry Falwell Scholarship) stamped on my school bill. Bless the Lord! God provided.

After graduation a major record label wanted to sign Transformation Crusade. So Chris, his new bride, Dorena, and the group headed to Nashville. Chris says,

> It wasn't long before our record label changed their minds and dropped us from our contract. I was dumbfounded and began to question God. I couldn't understand why He would let me come all the way to Nashville only to be rejected. What would a Baltimore kid with an affinity for Jesus and rap music do in country music USA? Obviously God had a plan.

After working at a metal shop in Tennessee for six months, Chris got a call from Christ Community Church in Franklin, Tennessee. The church of 4,000 needed an African American to lead the effort to reach into the minority community. He joined the staff as the pastoral intern of urban ministries and served the African American community for two and a half years, occasionally preaching at CCC.

Chris started a Bible study at his apartment complex to meet the ongoing needs of the neighborhood. Several families from his outreaches were interested. At the same time, several families from CCC wanted to help plant a new church. "It was obvious God was at work," Chris says. "He was bringing together two people groups."

God planted in Chris's heart the desire to start a multi-ethnic church. He began holding prayer meetings and taught on the diversity of the Jerusalem church and the church in Antioch. Others began to share the vision, and the first worship service of Strong Tower Bible Church was held in the YMCA aerobics room on September 3, 1995. Chris remembers "God moved in our midst and I was honored to pastor this special movement."

Strategy

Strong Tower Bible Church was planted as a multi-ethnic and multi-economic church led by God. Christ Community Church supported Chris for three years until the new church was more stable financially. Some of the CCC leaders even sat on the advisory board until Chris could recruit and train his own elders within the church.

The new congregation rented space from the YMCA because it was a neutral spot in town for a more diverse crowd. For ten years the congregation kept a trailer and storage sheds in the back of the YMCA. The group set up every Saturday night and tore down every Sunday afternoon before the YMCA opened. Over the years, the church used a high school, elementary school, and a rented office complex for Wednesday night Bible studies and programs. During that time the congregation also bought and sold a piece of property. Chris says,

> We decided that our ministry would not be dictated by
> a need to have our own building. We were intent on
> building the kingdom and not a church building. We
> also made a commitment not to go into debt doing the
> Lord's work, and if He had a building for us, it would
> pursue us. We also forged a philosophy that we were
> going to buy it in cash if it ever came down to that.
> We felt the Lord did in fact provide a facility for us
> through the YMCA, and we were not going to become
> distracted.

In 2006, Strong Tower Bible Church leased space at the Factory, a refurbished stove manufacturing plant that is home to restaurants, businesses, and artists. The congregation used the money from the property sale to make major renovations for office and children's ministry space at the Factory. Chris shares, "Before leaving the YMCA in 2005, we took a love offering one Sunday that totaled $137,000! Not bad for a church of about 400 people."

Since moving to the Factory, membership at Strong Tower has grown to just under 1,000 people. The congregation is also in the process of planting a church in Northern Virginia.

Successes

Strong Tower Bible Church has seen God knit people together from various races, economic standings, church backgrounds, cultural expressions, and political affiliations. The congregation is made up of blacks, whites, Native Americans, Asians, and Hispanics. There is ethnic diversity in leadership and staff. Strong Tower is a place where millionaires, low-income families, professional athletes, and people in the gospel music industry (like Natalie Grant, Selah, David and Nicole C. Mullen, and Toby Mac) worship together without distinction.

Pastor Chris says,

> We have maintained a wonderful and beautiful balance across the board. We have been good at keeping the main thing the main thing, and His name is Jesus. We have been successful at living in the balance of grace and truth. Our church has been a safe place for the abused and the struggling. We have recovered drug addicts and recovering drug addicts. Every year God brings in a financial surplus that we usually give to other ministries.

Strong Tower has seen God regularly save souls. And the church has sent teams and individuals to minister in Brazil, Ghana, Sudan, and Nigeria. As an action-oriented church, Strong Tower has helped hurricane victims in New Orleans, fleeing refugees in Darfur, and homeless people in Nashville.

Pastor Chris is proud of many programs in the church, including the women's ministry, children's ministry, student ministry, worship ministry, and pre-member's class.

The praise and worship ministry offers a variety of worship options on any given Sunday—a contemporary worship team, a gospel choir, traditional hymns, acapella singing, praise dance, drama, hip-hop music, funk, soul, and smooth jazz.

Struggles

Pastor Chris says lessons learned over the years include the importance of communication from the administration to the congregation on major decisions. He shares "We also struggled in handling personnel matters. Sometimes we hired people on heart and potential and not on heart and skill. We paid the price when we had to let them go."

But the greatest challenge currently at Strong Tower Pastor, Chris says, is recruiting and training lay ministry leaders in a more systematic, consistent, and holistic way. He said they are working on providing more direction, training, and vision for elders as well as empowering more men to lead.

Significance

Strong Tower Bible Church is a diverse church with a strong biblical foundation and emphasis. Pastor Chris explains it this way:

> The gospel of God's grace drives our church and not diversity, but our diversity is proof that the gospel is true. We are also unique because we have not made the acquisition of our own facilities a priority. We do not have debt as a ministry and we have been blessed to have eleven people on staff.

Statistics

Current membership is approximately 1,000 with an average Sunday attendance of 630. And the operating budget for 2008 was $1.4 million.

Structure

Strong Tower is a nondenominational, evangelical, elder-led, multidimensional body. The elder team comprises the senior pastor, the assistant pastor, the family pastor, a staff elder, and five lay elders. The church has eleven staff members, eight of them full-time. Every elder decision is made with a unanimous vote. The church also has a diaconate, comprising men and women who are extensions of the elder team to meet the needs of the body.

The church also has small groups called covenant groups, as well as interest groups that allow people to fellowship over various interests like bowling, reading, and movies. And the church has dances and concerts throughout the year.

Rather than a traditional Sunday school, Strong Tower offers the Christian Education Equipping Center, with classes for children, students, and adults in ten-week sessions or "mini-mesters." Classes cover books of the Bible, marriage, finances, racial issues, emotional disorders, health matters, and other topics. Between mini-mesters, the church holds three weeks of Celebration Sundays featuring prayer, worship, or other ministry focus.

Soul

Chris believes the heartbeat of Strong Tower "is the Word of God and real relationships." He says "keeping it real" begins in his role as pastor. He often shares his own shortcomings. He says this about the services:

> We are a vibrant and authentic church. We have so much life that it's hard to keep our services to an hour and a half. There's never a dull moment. Our mission

is to make disciples, and I believe we are doing that. Our vision is to experience and reproduce God's diverse kingdom, and we are blessed to have a taste of glory now. Our creed is "Church starts when you leave church." The gospel is just as much for the saved as it is for the lost.

Summary

In summary, Chris shares that a church planter must leave room for the Holy Spirit. He says that a church planter should plan but must not plan God out of the equation.

> Too often church planting is reduced to formulas and studies without prayer or dependence on the Holy Spirit. We want a move of God and not a cookie cutter ministry that is planned well but has no life.

He also gives this advice,

> Recognize that God stresses the function of the church over what form the church should take. God gives you freedom as you fulfill your function. Don't let other opinions, experiences, and perspectives dictate what you do or what kind of church you will have. Don't focus on having everything in order before you start.

> Don't determine success by numbers. You can do a lot with a few people. Don't define the church by the building it meets in. Don't feel like you have to have a traditional church building, and don't go into debt getting it. Make prayer an essential part of all that you do. Don't be afraid to do what's never been done. Don't appoint leaders quickly, but do appoint them. Never sacrifice your family for the ministry. Establish boundaries up front. Be a flexible wine skin for God to shape as he sees fit.

ABOUT THE CHURCH PLANTER—

Chris Williamson is the founder and Senior Pastor of Strong Tower Bible Church, begun in 1995 in Franklin, Tennessee.

Chris is a graduate of Liberty Baptist Theological Seminary. He attended in 1986–1990 and 1990–1992 and received a B.A. in Biblical Studies and Master of Arts in Religious Education.

Chris and his wife, Dorena, have been married since December 28, 1991. Chris was examined and ordained by Pastor McFarland in Portsmouth, Virginia, through his church, Calvary Evangelical Baptist Church.

Chapter 7
A Miracle in the
Middle of Nothing

"I was struck by the passion for worship and heart for the lost at C3 Church. As a matter of fact, those were the two things that blessed me the most. They are all about worship and making more worshippers through reaching the unchurched."

- Ed Stetzer

Story

Matt Fry was born in Tucson, Arizona, and grew up in Nashville, Tennessee. Matt attended Liberty University on a wrestling scholarship in 1983. When he was a freshman in college, God called him into full-time ministry. In 1985, Matt began serving a small Baptist church in Concord, Virginia, and in 1987 joined the youth staff of Thomas Road Baptist Church. After serving as a minister of students and Associate Pastor for various churches in Georgia, North Carolina, and South Carolina, Matt returned to Thomas Road Baptist and became the Pastor of Student Ministries in 1997.

While serving as Senior High Pastor at Thomas Road, he felt God beginning to burn a desire into his heart to start a church that would really reach people where they were living, where they were struggling, and where they were hurting. He picked up his Bible and began reading Matthew 9, where Jesus' heart broke in compassion for the people.

Jesus went through all the towns and villages, teaching in their synagogues, preaching the good news of the kingdom and healing every disease and sickness. When he saw the crowds, he had compassion on them, because they were harassed and helpless, like sheep without a shepherd. Then he said to his disciples, "The harvest is plentiful but the workers are few. Ask the Lord of the harvest, therefore, to send out workers into his harvest field." (Matthew 9:35–38 NIV)

Matt and his new bride, Martha, began sensing an overwhelming call to extend and demonstrate compassion to those in need. Initially, they were considering a church plant in Virginia Beach. But Martha's father asked the couple to prayerfully consider planting a church in Johnston County, North Carolina, outside the Raleigh–Durham area. Johnston County in the 1990s was one of the fastest growing areas in the country. The Frys felt a confirmation that this was what God wanted.

Matt shared his heart with Dr. Falwell. With the support and encouragement of Dr. Falwell and church leaders, Matt and Martha moved their family to Clayton, North Carolina.

Upon reading an article about the fifty most influential churches in America, Matt comments about the influence of Dr. Falwell in his life. He says Dr. Falwell was one who

> "Influenced me personally and resulted in a defining moment for my life and ministry. While attending Liberty University on an athletic scholarship with no plans for going into the ministry (or doing anything with God), I responded to a call from God to go into full-time ministry. I immediately began serving a local church and have continued to this day. Several years later, I served on Dr. Falwell's staff as the Senior High Pastor. During that time, God began to redirect my passion from students to families and church planting. As a result, we moved to North Carolina in 1998 and began our ministry at C3 Church. Although Dr. Falwell is on the list at No. 27 for 2006, I believe history will put him at the top of the list for the last century. Thanks,

Dr. Falwell. Because of you, I've learned to dream big dreams for God and have a heart and passion for the hurting and the lost."[19]

Matt had the vision. He had caught the vision in Lynchburg, as Dr. Falwell's faith prompted those around him to trust God to do great things. With the help of Dr. Falwell and the Student Ministries department of Thomas Road, high school students came to C3, provided worship and drama, and knocked on more than 2,000 doors, inviting the community to this new church.

The first time Matt preached at C3, September 1998, there were twenty-five adults in a cafeteria.

Strategy

On the kick-off Sunday service just a few weeks later, C3 had 167 in attendance.

This new and contemporary church, meeting in an old lunch room at the Cleveland Elementary School, was seeing people's lives being changed. As people began to attend, it became evident that there was a desperate need for a life-giving church in the area.

C3 strategy was to expose people to the Gospel through their weekend celebration, equip them through their Connect Groups, and have them experience God by serving one another through ministry teams.

Church attendance began to double every two years, and God began to bless this vibrant and exciting local church ministry.

C3 is building on the vision of providing "real hope for real people in a real world."

They accomplish this by exposing the Gospel of Jesus Christ to a lost and hurting world, equipping believers to be fully devoted followers of Jesus Christ, and experiencing ministry through the use of each individual's spiritual gifts and talents.

19   www.MattFry.com, Thanks for Impacting My Life . . . and Many Others, Matt Fry, July 15, 2006

The environment at C3 is welcoming, friendly, and relaxing, where people come dressed casually. Before or after the service, they encourage those attending to grab a cup of hot coffee and browse at their resource center called The Source.

C3's worship team plays energetic and passionate songs of worship. A fresh and modern style provides a meaningful way for believers to engage in worship and honor the Lord.

Each week, a relevant and vibrant message is designed to communicate what the Bible teaches, with practical applications to life.

C3 focuses on the importance of reaching every member of the family. For birth through fifth grade, C3 offers age-appropriate classes each weekend. Fusion is a middle school ministry, and Epic, the high school ministry, where students are challenged to live for Christ amid a challenging culture. All programming is designed to be relevant, fun, and life-changing.

Connect Groups were developed at C3 so people can build relationships with each other as they learn to live the life that God intended. These groups help to equip people to be fully devoted followers of Jesus Christ and are carried out through "connecting with God, connecting with others, and connecting with the community."

In 2000, the church purchased 47 acres—an old tobacco farm that would be the building site for a new worship center.

> In 2007, Yonat Shimron wrote in *The News & Observer*,
>
> On a two-lane country road near Clayton, a huge brick and steel edifice is rising out of the earth. It's not a shopping center or a school, through it resembles a little of both.
>
> It's a church, minus most of the trappings.
>
> When completed, it will have no stained-glass windows, pews or an organ—just a plain 98-foot steel cross to the

right of the entrance. Cleveland Community Church, known as "C3," is a contemporary church and its 82,618 square foot building is an example of the kind of church architecture being built across the south.[20]

Matt doesn't want the facility or worship to be a hindrance to those who have never attended church. He says, "We want this to be a place where people build community and relationships."

Christopher Lee of Willow Spring attended C3 for the first time when they moved into a new facility. He had watched the construction process take place and the building go up. "It doesn't look like a church," Lee says

Curiosity also captured Pam and Maurice Rozier who live in Clayton. Unlike others who attend the church for the first time, they were looking for a new church to join. "It's hard to find a church, where you're accepted, where you're around other Christians who have real lives and real problems," Pam Rozier says

Matt has placed a priority on people feeling welcomed and comfortable in the church. He says, "Christians can and should have fun. People will come to where there's life and where there's authenticity."[21]

Ed Stetzer, President of LifeWay Research, says about C3, "They have really thought through their mission, core beliefs and strategy. Front and center is an aim at being biblical while making Christ known and developing leaders."[22]

Reaching those who don't know Christ continues to be a priority at C3. Arriving on the campus of the church, people are drawn to the 98-foot cross as the fulcrum of the buildings. Interestingly, the spiraling cross corresponds to the year the church began, 1998. The foundation of the cross illustrates the desire of C3 to reach people with the life-changing message of Christ. In July 2007, "Rocks for the Cross" was an

---

20   The News & Observer, *21st-Centruy Church: Vast, Plain, Informal,* Yonat Shimron, November 11, 2007

21   The News & Observer, *God, Country and Dale Junior,* John Murawski, July 7, 2008

22   *Sunday in Raleigh Durham,* EdStetzer.com, December 6, 2008

opportunity for church members to write the name of someone who did not know Christ on a rock and place it in the foundation of the 98-foot cross. That faith act has continued to develop as stories of the "rock names" have come to know Christ as Savior.

In 2009, Pastor Matt presented an ever-growing vision for C3. Their vision is to expose people to the Gospel, equip them through their Connect Groups, and have them experience God by serving. They have added one more element to their vision: expand the work of the ministry of C3 to new territory.

The expansion of ministry consists of several new elements. Fry plans to start a fourth service that will continue to develop the ministry of C3. With current service being held on Saturday evenings at 6 p.m., Sunday morning at 9:15 a.m. and 11:15 a.m., C3 will add a Saturday service at 4 p.m. Pastor Fry asked for "300" warriors to help populate this new service, and 400 signed up.

C3 is also adding new worship environments. C3 Café is an alternate worship venue presented in a very casual and relaxed environment. They expect an average attendance of over seventy new people per week.

They continue to offer their live feed of all services through C3's website, www.c3church.com. Listeners have been recorded from around the world, seeing and experiencing the ministry of C3.

C3 has a desire to plant a new campus in Raleigh. In analyzing their current attendance, 275 families attend C3 from the Raleigh area, almost 40 miles away, and over 30,000 new families move into the Raleigh area each year. In order to address this ever-growing area of ministry, Matt is encouraging 200 "warriors" from C3 to go and help build this new church campus.

C3 will continue to expand their vision by partnering with several other ministries to plant churches throughout the country. They are on target to plant fifty churches in the next twelve-month period.

Successes

Worship is a key element in the ministry of C3. Stetzer says, "I was struck by the passion for worship and heart for the lost at C3 Church. As a matter of fact, these are the two things that blessed me the most. They are all about worship and making more worshippers through reaching the un-churched. They have grown rapidly (to 3,000 in weekly attendance) and have plans to continue to reach out and grow."[23]

Matt agrees with the importance of worship. He writes, "It's so awesome when you have a worship service planned and God steps in and just moves in a powerful way. It seems like every time we gather together for worship, God is up to something big and special."[24]

Another area of impact at C3 is the focus on prayer and fasting. In 2009, Pastor Matt and his wife, Martha, began the year by joining over 300 other churches in a twenty-one-day period of prayer and fasting. Matt writes on his blog, "I can't think of a better way to begin the year, and I am praying that the result will be that more lives will be changed this year than ever before."

Many in C3 expressed an enthusiasm and expectation as to what God was going to do in the 21 days. Another attendee of CS, Scott says, "I'm excited about what God is going to do in the next 21 days. God is awesome!"

That sentiment was prevalent throughout the church as hundreds joined together each Wednesday morning at 6 a.m. to worship, seek God and petition Him to do great things in the church.

Prayer and fasting have been a characteristic of C3 since its beginning. In 2006, Matt and Martha asked C3 to join them in forty-eight hours of prayer and fasting before moving into a new building. Matt writes, "We are asking God to prepare our hearts and to use us to make a difference."[25]

---

23   ibid
24   www.MattFry.com, WOW!, Matt Fry, August 4, 2006
25   www.MattFry.com, Thanks for Impacting My Life . . . and Many Others, Matt Fry, July 15, 2006

Bill Bright of Campus Crusade saidof fasting, "I believe the power of fasting as it relates to prayer is the spiritual atomic bomb that our Lord has given us to destroy the strongholds of evil and usher in a great revival and spiritual harvest around the world."

The emphasis on prayer runs through every area of the church. Matt shares about a youth weekend,

> What an amazing weekend … our prayer was that this would be the most dynamic experience our students have ever seen. And God did more than we asked. The Youth Quest teams, led by Chris Pope, did an amazing job leading the small groups and the rallies. One memory that will never leave my mind, was the sight on Sunday night at the end of the service as Adam McCain asked the students if they wanted to be prayed for to make a difference (and not waste their life), to come forward and one of the C3 leaders would pray over them. Over a hundred students literally ran to the front to be prayed for as the Youth Quest band led us in worship. The whole weekend was filled with "God Moments" … Spontaneous times of prayer, worship, and responding to God … students on their knees crying out to God.[26]

In moving into their new facility, Pastor Matt and Martha asked the church to join them in prayer. The construction was done, the process was complete, but that was only part of the job. He writes,

> As we have been busy getting everything prepared for the new building I felt God say to me "Be sure and have your heart prepared." Having the 'physical' prepared is important, but the most important part is to make sure that we are 'spiritually' prepared.
>
> Joshua 3:5: *"Joshua told the people, 'Consecrate yourselves, for tomorrow the Lord will do amazing things among you'" (NIV)*. For those that are available, we are going

---

26   www.MattFry.com, Can You Believe It, Matt Fry, December 21, 2007

to meet at the church on Saturday night at 5 p.m. for a time of prayer. Will you join with Martha and me in praying for this Sunday and all that God is going to do?[27]

This abandonment to worship, coupled with the commitment to prayer and fasting, has developed a sense of purpose and acceptance in Pastor Matt's calling and ministry. He has discovered the freedom to be the type of pastor that fits his design.

Much of this freedom has been cultivated from his willingness to be a humble and teachable servant. He illustrates this by writing,

> I had the privilege of spending some time with a few pastors the last few days. These guys are some amazing leaders that are making a huge impact around the world. I love hearing what God is doing in other churches and other cultures. To be honest, I wasn't really interested in getting on another airplane and being away from my family and my home … but it was a tremendous time of connecting with other leaders and learning from their successes … and mistakes. I am reminded of Proverbs 27:17, *"As iron sharpens iron, so one man sharpens another."*
>
> **I need to learn from others and it is a blessing to have relationships with other great leaders. I'm so thankful that I have men that build me up and that make me a better person and friend.**[28]

Struggles

With many successes, there are just as many dark days of denial and doubt. Pastor Matt writes about one of those times:

---

27   www.MattFry.com, I Still Have A Lot to Learn, Matt Fry, November 8, 2007

28   www.MattFry.com, The Revolution Has Begun, Matt Fry, February 26, 2007

About four years ago, after a difficult few months of ministry, and the typical challenges that come with planting a church, I was tempted to throw in the towel of ministry, or at least as a Senior Pastor. I took a mini-sabbatical and went to Charleston, SC, and spent some time with Pastor Greg. He took time out of his busy schedule to spend time with some "no name" young pastor from North Carolina.

He listened to me whine and complain … and then he encouraged me to hang in there. He explained that what I was experiencing was part of the challenges that come with being a Senior Pastor and taking a church through growth barriers.[29]

One of those growth barriers becomes evident in finding leadership for developing areas of ministry. Matt comments,

Most churches have a great resource of leadership potential from those who have been involved in church, but never served. At C3, the majority of our people have never been involved in church and they don't know what it means to be a leader or to care for part of the flock. We need to teach them to grow spiritually … and then help them find a place to serve that compliments their spiritual journey. The biggest mistake we can make is to put someone in a position of leadership when they are not ready.

In the process of developing believers through a growth and discipleship process, Matt believes that the church's emphasis on prayer and fasting has been a key.

Most new Christians crave the opportunity to pray and fast. They don't know any different. If it helps them grow closer to God and see God do incredible things, they are all about it. After all, their lives have been totally transformed by Jesus Christ. If He can do that

---

29   www.MattFry.com, 15 Days and Counting, Matt Fry, August 25, 2006

... what else can He do if they commit to knowing
Him better through self sacrifice and worship.

New and growing leaders are also encouraged to build relationships
with others through C3's Connect Groups. These become a place where
people learn to live the life that God intended. They equip people to be
fully devoted followers of Jesus Christ by connecting with Him, with
each other, and with the community.

Another challenge in building the ministries of C3 is in the
uniqueness of the ministry itself. Being located in the Raleigh Triangle
area of North Carolina, many are "indoctrinated" with the image of
"church." This Bible-belt area is steeped in tradition and liturgy. As
Matt and Martha have created nontraditional approaches to ministry,
many have been hesitant and questioned this new church. Matt writes,
"Blazing a new trail of ministry has been a challenge because we are so
'outside the box' of what most people think church is ... this includes
our size, our style, and facility and even our passion."

As C3 has become more committed to helping the hurting and
disenfranchised in their community, the more the barriers of tradition
have come down. Through special friend Sundays and community
outreaches to provide backpacks to school children, people's lives have
been changed and transformed. C3 has become a place of hope and
healing.

A visionary often faces growth blocks in the area of staying focused
to the vision and mission that was embraced during the foundational
years of ministry growth. Often a visionary will sense God's leading in
refining the vision and expanding the mission. The challenge will come
when leadership adjustments are necessary to accommodate visionary
development and execution. Visionary leaders need to continually
communicate the vision and articulate the "why" and "what" of God's
development of their ministry. Matt accomplishes this through sharing
the purpose of C3, reviewing what God has done, and setting the
course as to what God wants to continue to do.

Significance

The impact of C3 on the local community of Raleigh is noteworthy. As a rapidly growing church and ministry, C3 has identified itself as a church that expects excellence in all that it does.

Looking back at the influence of Dr. Falwell, Matt recalls the clarion call to practice excellence in every aspect of ministry. From the facilities of C3 to the programming, a desire to represent the Creator of all is foundational. Doing your best and being your best provides a clear picture of who God is to those searching for answers.

Whether it's a children's program that is just beginning, an outdoor baptism, worship, or a new message series, there is an emphasis on getting it right and making it right.

After speaking at C3, Ed Stetzer writes,

> I was impressed with the fact that they immediately evaluated the service after we were done. They discussed everything about it, made changes, and sought to make it better. I don't see that much in churches—and I think it made the services on Sunday better.

It is also a church that is authentic and real. It's simple: Matt and Martha continue to focus on the basic principles of the Christian walk, protecting the purpose and passion of the ministry from too many programs.

God is doing a great work, and Matt continues to emphasize that it is God doing it and not him. During the construction of C3's newest facility, Matt recalls a tender time with his family. He writes,

> It was amazing to see our new worship center and children's area filled with families writing verses on the concrete floor. One of the scriptures that Martha and I wrote on the floor is Ephesians 3:20–21,
>
> *"Now to Him who is able to do immeasurably more than all we ask or imagine, according to His power that is at work within us, to Him be glory in the church and in*

Christ Jesus throughout all generations, forever and ever! Amen."

One of the highlights for me was experiencing this with my family.... An experience I will never forget.[30]

C3 is also a church that believes in shared ministry leadership between husband and wife.

If Matt is the evangelist, Martha is the discipler. If Matt is the visionary, Martha is the implementer. If Matt desires to worship at the throne of God, Martha is the one who opens the door. They truly complement each other in ministry roles.

Martha oversees the creative arts and worship ministries of C3. It is common to see her on stage leading worship and assisting her husband by leading people into the throne room of God through praise and worship.

She also gives leadership to the Connect Groups. This is one of the more critical areas of ministry that provides believers with the tools to grow in Christ and prepares them to be fully devoted followers of Christ.

Martha understands that the ministry is not about her and not about Matt. She is quick to admit that she is amazed that God would use them to build this church. Her favorite verse summarizes her gratitude and dependence upon Christ.

Brothers, think of what you were when you were called. Not many of you were wise by human standards; not many were influential; not many were of noble birth. But God chose the foolish things of the world to shame the wise; God chose the weak things of the world to shame the strong. He chose the lowly things of this world and the despised things—and the things that are not—to nullify the things that are, so that no one may boast before Him. It is because

---

30   www.MattFry.com, New Building and Writing Scripture on the Floor, Matt
     Fry, August 8, 2007

> *of Him that you are in Christ Jesus, who has become for*
> *us wisdom from God—that is, our righteousness, holiness*
> *and redemption. Therefore, as it is written: "Let him who*
> *boasts boast in the Lord." (1 Corinthians 1:26–31)*

Matt understands the value of shared ministry and the importance of having a spouse who serves and sacrifices with him in the work of C3. Matt writes, "I am so blessed to have a wife that serves with me in ministry. She's not only a great leader, but an awesome communicator." He continues, "I am amazed at the team that God has surrounded me with. Thanks, Martha, for being a great mom, wife, and partner in ministry!"

One of the challenges this shared ministry relationship brings about is the classic struggle between a visionary leader and those who implement the vision. In an interview with Matt and Martha, she states,

> As staff, we need to find the balance of trusting the visionary pastor with the dream that God has given and being responsible for the resources that God has given us to accomplish that dream. We need to make sure we are trusting God for the details just as much as Matt trusted God for the dream. If God has given Matt a vision … after he has prayed, sought God and received the faith … we, as his support team, need to get alone with God and find that same faith to accomplish the vision.

When asked if she has ever second-guessed Matt, she replied,

> Yes. I need to remember to be supportive as a staff member and as a wife. Sometimes that line is hard to maintain. Because we are so comfortable with each other, we both tend to "press the envelope." I really need to come to the point of knowing that Matt has said it … he believes it is from God … now I have to be honoring, patient and ready to submit.

When prompted with the question, "Is it easier to submit as a wife or a staff member?" Martha replied, "It's much harder to submit as a staff member than as a wife."

One strategy that has developed in their relationship is that Matt and Martha both see a growing need to intentionally pursue each other—as husband and wife, and as partners in the grace of God.

Matt states, "I have purposefully come to the place in my life where I need to pursue Martha with the same passion and intensity that I have for C3. She is my bride ... just like the church is Christ's bride. Jesus was unashamedly passionate about His bride ... even to the point of giving of His own comforts, His own desires, and His own feelings. I need to be of the same intent with my bride, my partner in life and my partner in ministry."

Summary

In looking back, Matt stresses the importance of clearly understanding the call to plant a church. It requires steps of obedience and faith. At first, the steps of faith are very small, yet they are steps that each person has to take. As the journey continues, the steps of faith become more frequent and larger. The more you learn to trust God, the more you need to trust God. Before long, you're able to look back and see where God—and only God—has taken you.

Matt encourages that as church planters begin, they plant with a team. He also emphasizes the importance of planting with a network that will provide training, coaching and mentoring.

Most recently, C3 Church has become a multi-site ministry by establishing a campus in Raleigh. The two campuses, C3 Clayton and C3 Raleigh, continue to reach the Triangle area of North Carolina with six weekend services.

Soul

A church that is passionate for God in their worship, in their prayer, in their commitment, in their service: This passion is what Matt and Martha identify as the soul of C3.

A member recalls a powerful story at one of the C3 services:

> What an amazing service tonight! What an inspiration to see a place jam packed with Christians raising their arms, worshipping and praising Jesus. Tonight's sermon by Matt and praying by Martha was so heartfelt. And the music was moving! And to see all those people and kids publicly declaring their faith.
>
> Pastor Matt and the rest of you clearly have God working through all of you. You have all made such an impression in my life and my family's life, and future generations, I can't thank you enough. I cannot imagine what my life would be like without Jesus. Thank God I do not have to.
>
> Thank you for the ultimate miracle of salvation and my wife recommitting her faith as you are definitely part of it including our baptisms. My father getting saved, having a sense of comfort knowing my mom is in heaven after her passing in April and knowing that one day I will join her and tonight committing to raise our children under the guidance of God.
>
> I will never forget the day I drove into the C3 parking lot and met you and walked inside. It was the beginning of an amazing journey! Keep up the awesome work! I can't wait for the first Wednesday in the new building and the day we have 2,000 people getting crazy for Jesus! I can already see it ...

Statistics and Structure

In January 2009, C3 has an attendance of 3,200 per week. As a church, they occupy an 82,618-square-foot facility located on 47 acres in Johnston County, North Carolina.

Cleveland Community Church (C3) began with partnerships with Liberty Baptist Fellowship, Association of Related Churches (ARC), North Carolina Baptist Association, and EQUIP. They currently have 27 paid staff with over 800 volunteers.

C3 is a pastor-led church.

ABOUT THE CHURCH PLANTER—

Matt Fry is the founding and Lead Pastor of the C3 Church (Cleveland Community Church) in Clayton, North Carolina (www.c3church.com) and Raleigh, North Carolina. C3 is a contemporary church serving the Triangle area of North Carolina. C3 has been built on the vision of providing "real hope for real people in a real world."

A recognized leader in the church planning movement, Matt serves on the leadership team of ARC (Association of Related Churches). He posts weekly on his blog, at www.mattfry.com.

Matt is a graduate of Liberty University in Lynchburg, Virginia (B.S., Youth Ministry). He was ordained at Bethany Baptist Church in Snellville, Georgia, in 1989.

Married since 1992, Matt and Martha have three children—Gloria, Caroline, and Caleb.

Chapter 8
A Family of Church Planting

"I heard Max Lucado make a statement that changed the course of our church and my life. He said, 'It's not about me, and it's not about you. God does not exist to make much of us. Instead, we exist to make much of Him.' After hearing him speak, I left the conference, drove to Laguna Beach, sat down on a bench overlooking the Pacific Ocean, and wrote a new mission statement for my life. 'My purpose is to pursue such intimacy with Christ that the glory of God is revealed through every area of my life.' On that day, I gave God a blank check."

- Brian Bloye, 2003

As you drive down Hiram-Acworth Highway, you pass a number of churches and chapels. However, Paulding County once posted an unchurched rate of 93.7 percent. On the edge of the county, just down the highway on the corner of East Paulding Drive, is the location of West Ridge Church, a twelve-year-old church plant and a force for change in the communities of Paulding County and the surrounding area. In 2007, the county's unchurched rate was reduced to 88 percent.

This incredible church and humble pastor have written a story of God's provision, leadership, and grace as they reach over 4,000 people each week.

Story

Brian Bloye was born August 22, 1965, in Highland Park, Michigan. When Brian was a young boy, the Bloyes bought the flower shop in Detroit and began a family business. Brian recalls spending most of his holidays in a flower shop.

His father was saved in 1976 during a time when his mother filed for divorce. The salvation of Brian's dad saved his marriage. In 1978, his dad surrendered to a call to preach. In June 1980, the family moved to Arlington, Texas, where his dad enrolled in Arlington Baptist College.

Brain was saved at very young age and came to an understanding of the salvation experience at a Billy Graham Crusade on November 28, 1978. A year later, he surrendered to full-time ministry at a winter camp in northern Michigan.

In 1983, Mr. Bloye graduated from Bible college. It was the same year Brian graduated from high school.

In July 1983, the Bloye family moved to Boynton Beach, Florida, to plant a church.

In December 1984, Brian enrolled at Arlington Baptist College to study pastoral ministry and subsequently transferred to Dallas Baptist University where he played baseball and studied communications.

After watching his dad struggle while planting a church in Florida, Brian decided he was done with ministry. He relates how God began to get his attention in the spring of 1985. He shares,

> One night in the spring of 1985, I was lying on the couch in my living room in Texas watching the *Old-Time Gospel Hour*. I have no idea why. I listened to Dr. Falwell talk about Liberty. I sat there and watched for a while and knew in my heart that I was supposed to go to school in Lynchburg. I called several of my friends that night on the phone and told them I was going to Liberty and they should transfer and go with me. I came to Liberty with seven other friends from Texas.

That summer, Brian's parents moved back to Michigan to start a second church, Grace Baptist Church. Brian spent the summer in Michigan helping get the church off the ground.

In August 1985, Brian enrolled at Liberty University as a junior and graduated with a degree in communications in 1988. Brian wanted to play baseball at LU, but in 1986, he tore the labrum in his pitching shoulder and never played baseball again.

In October 1987, Thomas Road Baptist Church hosted a Super Conference featuring Dr. John MacArthur. MacArthur spoke on Isaiah 6. That night Brian re-surrendered his life to full-time ministry.

In January 1988, Brian enrolled in LBTS to begin work on a master's degree. A year later, he accepted a job as the full-time student pastor at First Baptist Church in Pemberton, New Jersey. He continued his graduate work and enrolled as a full-time student at Biblical Theological Seminary in Hatfield, Pennsylvania. Brian writes about his time in graduate school, "My commute to school four days a week was one and a half hours one-way. It was a crazy time in my life."

During the next few years, Brian went through two broken engagements. One was after a five-year relationship; the other ended twenty-eight days before the scheduled wedding date.

> In June 1991, Brian received a life-changing call. He relates,

> I received a phone call from Jerry Falwell asking me if I was interested in coming back to Lynchburg to be the middle school pastor at Thomas Road Baptist Church (TRBC). After much prayer, I accepted the offer. I left New Jersey one class short of a master's degree in Old Testament studies and one semester short of my MDiv from Biblical. I finally finished my Masters of Divinity from Liberty Baptist Theological Seminary in 1993 and walked in 1994.

Brian served as the middle school pastor at TRBC from 1991 to 1993 and was ordained in May 1992. He then led the high school ministry from 1993 to 1997, oversaw all student ministries, and taught student ministry at LBTS in 1995.

In 1991 Brian was introduced by a group of middle school students to Amy Mills. Amy was a new seventh-grade teacher at Liberty Christian Academy. They were married on December 19, 1992. They have two sons, John Taylor and Zachary.

In the fall of 1995, God allowed Brian and Amy to go through a time of wrestling and seeking concerning God's will and direction for their lives. After almost nine years of working with students, Brian felt God was calling them to something else. They didn't know what. They felt God leading their hearts away from Lynchburg but just didn't know where.

Brian recalls the struggle:

One night in November 1995, Amy and I were up late talking about this wrestling that we were going through. She asked me, "If you could do anything right now in ministry, what would you do?" I replied, "What would you think about planting a church?" She answered, "You mean with no people, no money, no building?" I said, "Yeah! Doesn't it sound exciting?" She answered, "Just the thought of it makes my stomach turn ... but you know that I am up for whatever God has for us."

In January, 1996 Brian and his dad went to a Promise Keepers Pastors Conference at the Georgia Dome in Atlanta. He was still wrestling with God. On the second day of the conference, Chuck Swindoll spoke from Isaiah 6. Once again, this significant passage began to work in Brian's heart. He writes,

Even though there were 42,000 pastors in the Georgia Dome, it was like He was speaking directly to me. I knew that this was going to be a moment of decision for me. Swindoll told the story of God humbling Isaiah, Isaiah repenting, and then God calling him out. "Who will go for me? Who will I send?" I was under heavy conviction.

After Swindoll preached, Jack Hayford came out and led all 42,000 pastors in the old hymn "Holy, Holy, Holy." It was unbelievable. Everyone stood and sang with hands raised, except me. I was fighting God. I didn't want to leave student ministry, and I didn't really want to leave Lynchburg. However, I knew God was calling me to surrender. Finally, I stood and raised my hands and told God, "Here I am God, I will go, send me."

I left my seat and went down near the stage area of the Georgia Dome. There were probably twenty-five other people lying prostrate on the ground. I fell down on my face and said, "God, here I am, tell me what you want me to do." At that moment, God put Joshua 3:5 on my heart: "sanctify yourselves, for tomorrow I will do amazing things amongst you."

When he returned home from Lynchburg, Brian told Amy that God wanted them to leave student ministries and Lynchburg. When she asked where they were going, Brian said, "I don't know, but it's going to be exciting."

In the spring of 1996, Brian spoke with various churches all over the country. Nothing seemed to fit.

In March 1996, Brian and Amy made an appointment to meet with Dr. Falwell. Although they had known Dr. Falwell since 1985, they were nervous with the thought of the meeting. Brian relates,

I had worked for him for five years. He treated Amy and me like his own kids. I said, "Doc, Amy and I feel that God is leading us away from student ministry and away from Lynchburg." He said, "Where are you going?" I said, "We don't know, we just know with all of our hearts that God is leading us to do something different that what we're doing now." Dr. Falwell asked us if there was anything he could do to talk us into staying. I said, "No, we truly believe God is in this decision." He said, "Why don't you pick a major city that is fast growing and go start a contemporary style church?" He suggested the Washington DC area. We talked for a while about what that might look like and then he prayed with us.

As we walked to our car, I looked at Amy and said, "Well, what do you think about what he just said in there?" She replied, "Church planting doesn't that sound exciting?" After months of praying and searching for answers, God had melted our hearts together, and we finally knew what He was asking us to do ... plant a church.

Brian and Amy went home and put a map of the U.S. on the table and begin to pray about where to go. In April 1996, they were visiting with family in Dallas, Georgia, just outside Atlanta. At lunch, they were asked some questions about their church planting plans. Family members suggested that they consider Paulding County, Georgia. Brian's response was "Why in the world does Atlanta need another church?"

As they drove back home to Lynchburg, Amy and Brian could not stop talking about Paulding County. They did not want to move to Georgia. However, they couldn't stop thinking about it. When they got home, Brian got on the Internet and began to research Paulding County. He found out that it was the seventh fastest growing county in the country and 93.7 percent unchurched. God began working in his heart.

In the summer of 1996, Brian was speaking at a Go Tell Camp, along with Dr. Johnny Hunt, Pastor of Woodstock Baptist Church in the Atlanta area. Dr. Hunt approached Brian and introduced himself. Although Brian did not know Dr. Hunt, he asked him if he knew where Paulding County was. Brian was told it was a few counties over from Dr. Hunt's church in Woodstock, Georgia. Brian related that he was going to move there to start a church. Dr. Hunt said, "Why don't you let us help you?" At that point, Brian knew he was moving to Atlanta.

Brian talks about the start of this journey:

> In the fall of 1996, I began to call tons of friends that I knew in the ministry world to ask them if they would be interested in moving with us to Georgia. Nearly every one of them kindly turned us down. However, three guys told me they were interested; Steve Veale, a friend of mine from college and his wife, Christie. They were on staff at a church in Boca Raton, Florida. Dave Cole, a friend of mine from seminary, and his wife, Chris, were on staff with Kansas City Youth for Christ. And, Paul Richardson, who was engaged to Angela, also came on board. He was a student of mine at TRBC. These guys are all still with me. Amy and I left Lynchburg June 1, 1997. Our staff families joined us in Georgia in July 1997.

Looking back on his experience at Thomas Road and Liberty, Brian writes,

> My time in Lynchburg taught me to dream big. It helped me to realize that with God, all things are possible. When we finally launched West Ridge Church on September 7, 1997, we had 251 people in attendance. It blew us away. We started West Ridge with three full-time employees and one bi-vocational staff member.

Strategy

Months before moving to Paulding County, the three team members combined their mailing lists and sent out over 500 letters to friends and family asking them to support this new endeavor. Their goal was to raise $185,000 over a two-year period.

Throughout that summer they spent day after day knocking on doors telling people about a church that was coming to the area. They also met every Thursday night with a growing core group of people that were interested in the new church.

During those early years, Brian writes,

> Our strategy when we started was to start a church with
> multiple staff, build a core group, and to create a buzz.
> We wanted to market West Ridge in such a way that
> people HAD to come and check it out. We showed
> up at every county "happening" there was with free
> balloons and free water (with the WRC logo on them)
> to promote the church. We knocked on thousands of
> doors and handed out brochures. We brought in youth
> groups and college students to canvass neighborhoods
> for us. We blanketed the community with a program
> called, *Acts of Kindness*. We knew that we were bringing
> a very contemporary approach to church to a VERY
> traditional, religious area, so we had to come with the
> love of Jesus.

And God began to bless. They met for three years (1997–2000) at
Vaughan Elementary School where they grew to about 900.

In September 2000, they moved to East Paulding High School,
where they stayed for five years and grew to more than 2,800. Their
growth caused them to occupy nearly the entire school. They had three
services meeting in a high school gymnasium. Brian recalls using every
bit of space:

> Our children's ministry met in a cafeteria, our students
> met in band and choral rooms, and our preschool met
> in classrooms down two hallways. We had four setup
> and teardown teams. God blessed our hard work and
> used our volunteers.

Planting other churches also became an aspect of West Ridge. Brian
writes,

> When we moved here, we really didn't think about
> planting other churches. It wasn't on our radar.
> However, in 2001 we decided that we would start
> supporting church planters around Atlanta and the
> U.S. We quickly moved from supporting churches

financially, to supporting them with people and other resources.

In the midst of all the incredible growth and work, Brian needed to find some time to refresh and seek God's direction. That time came in the summer of 2003. He writes,

> In July 2003, I took my first sabbatical. I was tired and worn out from the first five years of West Ridge. I attended a worship pastor's conference at Saddleback Church in Southern California. On the last day of the conference, I heard Max Lucado make a statement that changed the course of our church and my life. He said, "It's not about me, and it's not about you. God does not exist to make much of us. Instead, we exist to make much of Him." After hearing him speak, I left the conference, drove to Laguna Beach, sat down on a bench overlooking the Pacific Ocean, and wrote a new mission statement for my life. "My purpose is to pursue such intimacy with Christ that the glory of God is revealed through every area of my life." On that day, I gave God a blank check.

He continues to talk about the impact of that moment:

Several things transpired, over time, out of that monumental time with God. From now on this would no longer be about me; this would now be all about God and His Glory. This would no longer be about one church; this would be about many churches. We would no longer take exposure trips to countries; we would strategically enter countries to change them. We would no longer do *Acts of Kindness* in Atlanta to promote West Ridge Church; we would do them to transform the community with the love of Christ.

In August 2003, West Ridge bought fifty acres of property across the street from the high school that was revealed to Brian during a forty-day fast. A few years later, they would buy twelve additional acres and two houses. Dr. Jerry Falwell and Dr. Johnny Hunt came to dedicate the land in 2004.

In December 2005, West Ridge moved into a 104,000–square-foot facility, including modular trailers. Dr. Falwell and Jonathan Falwell came to dedicate the new building in January 2006.

Successes

West Ridge models success by the changes in lives as opposed to numbers and attendance. There are several areas that are a highlight.

The Spiritual Growth of People: Since the beginning of West Ridge Church, several thousand people have come to know Christ as their Savior. In addition, well over 1,500 people have been baptized since 1997. In January 2008, Brian taught about the importance of baptism and spontaneously asked if anyone would obey and follow the Lord in baptism. As he walked to the baptistery in his clothes, 132 responded and were baptized on the spot.

Community Outreach and Service: In 2006 and 2007, West Ridge completed two complete home makeovers in their community. In 2006, West Ridge started a ministry on Tuesday Night called Tuesday Night Life. They currently minister to more than 500 people who attend for Divorce Care, Grief Share, Window of Hope, Celebrate Recovery, Financial Peace University, and other helping groups. In 2007, West Ridge ministered to over 750 families at Thanksgiving and Christmas.

In 2008, Bloye started a nonprofit called Engage Atlanta where churches around the Atlanta area can come together for community transformation. In August 2008, eight churches came together, with over 3,000 people participating, to do over 250 projects over one weekend in their community. To end the weekend, they had a huge celebration in a Sam's Club parking lot with over 6,000 people in attendance.

Also, in 2008 West Ridge ministered to over 1,500 families at Thanksgiving and Christmas. All of the families came to the campus and received food, toys, and other gifts.

Church Planting: West Ridge shared support of their first three church plants in 2001. In 2004, they launched their own first church plant. Since that point they have planted over thirty churches with the 2010 goal set at fifty churches. In 2005, West Ridge launched WRC School of Church Planting which currently trains and equips prospective church planters. In 2007, West Ridge started a church-planting network, Net 35, where their own church plants and others are investing in new plants. Additionally, West Ridge is invited to be a founding partner of Vision 360, a church planting movement started by Al Weiss, President of Worldwide Operations for Disney Theme Parks, Resorts, and Cruise Lines.

Cross Cultural Missions: In 2007, West Ridge built and planted House of Prayer in San Francisco de Palo, Cuba. In 2008, a team was sent to Burkina Faso, Africa, to investigate the opportunities to not only work in this impoverished nation, but to start a church planting movement. Also, in 2008, World Help was given $40,000 to build a safe house in Uganda.

Struggles

With rapid growth there comes constant evaluation and change. This often occurs as struggles are evaluated and new strategies are implemented.

Over the last few years, as the economy has gotten worse, West Ridge's finances have struggled. They are also currently understaffed for all they feel God has called them to do.

Brian faced some major events in 2004. At that time, the major oversight of the staff had been delegated, and staffing issues became a concern. In addition, Brian suffered a tragic loss.

He shares from his heart:

In 2004 I lost my dad in a rafting accident. For about a year and half, I really struggled to get through my grief. It caused me to allow the vision of the church to drift. I simply did not have the energy and focus to lead strongly. From 2006 to 2007, I had to painfully take the church back over and get it back on course. It cost me staff members, friendships, and a handful of people.

In subsequent years, clarity of vision was regained by a reevaluation of purpose and mission.

Brian writes,

One of the biggest changes we have made as a church is to place a major emphasis on the Kingdom of God. We are focusing much of our speaking and strategy around helping people live out their Kingdom purpose and calling. We have T-shirts in our café that say, It s Not About Me. We are challenging our people to get financially, spiritually, and physically healthy, so that if God were to call them to be part of a church planting team, they would be ready. We want people to be ready if God called them to go to Africa. We want them to be ready if God were to have them resign from what they are doing to start a nonprofit. We want to go from being a "Catch and Keep Church" to being a "Catch and Release Church."

THIS IS NOT ABOUT BUILDING OUR KINGDOM, IT'S ABOUT BUILDING HIS!

In the area of starting new ministries, Brian shares,

We have learned a great lesson over the years about not starting ministries before their time. We have, in the past, started things without the right leadership and strategy in place, and it has hurt us. Now we only start things if they fall within one of our four activities: Love, Grow, Serve, Share. We also must have the right strategy and leadership in place, as well as confirmation from God.

Clarification was also needed in the rapid growth of the church planting strategy and emphasis. The quality of the church planter was beginning to be less than what was desired. The quality control of the product began to decline. Brian writes, "We no longer give significant support to church plants that do not come from out of our School of Church Planting. We did this early on, and it caused us to invest in some things that were not as successful as we had hoped they would have been."

Significance

West Ridge Church was created to reach the 93.7 percent of Paulding County, Georgia, that was unchurched.

The worship at West Ridge Church is considered Spirit-filled, contemporary, and modern. It's a rock, southern rock feel. The eighty-minute service is seeker friendly, but geared towards believers.

The preaching is expository and topical. The lead pastor strategically plans topical studies, character studies, book studies, and doctrinal studies throughout the calendar year.

West Ridge is a church of small groups, not a church that sees small groups as another program of the church. Most everything they do is done through small groups. They have over 100 small groups for adults. They are divided up and coached by geographical zones.

The local outreach is done through relationships by the personal elements of investing and inviting, as well as special events. They have major outreach events scheduled through the year including Easter, RUSH Student Camp, Surge Sports Camp, Western Jamboree, Dinner in December, and Christmas Eve.

Summary

The following are 25 "lessons" that Brian feels are critically important for church planters.

1. You need to have strategic and renewal plans for the Big 3: Rehydrate, Replenish, Refuel

2. Establish your leadership values early. Don't apologize for them.

3. Set boundaries for your life and your family. Lead your family before you lead the church.

4. Define early on what you do and don't do.

5. Lead leaders. Always be on the lookout for new leaders. Spend your best time investing in leaders.

6. Be clear about how you make decisions.

7. Don't allow yourself to get bogged down in the muck. Do not spend your best hours with people who will drain and waste your time.

8. Always be out ahead of your people spiritually.

9. Know your besetting sin, and have a plan to keep it in check.

10. Have a plan for discouragement. Exercise, God time, healthy escapes, and having fun.

11. Set up a system around you that complements your leadership style yet provides accountability.

12. Work on your strengths; let someone else fill in where you're weak.

13. Be very clear about your directives.

14. Understand the price of leadership early, and don't whine about it. Leadership can be lonely.

15. Be careful what you promise early on; it may come back to bite you.

16. Do not sacrifice the spiritual—stay desperate for God.

17. Do not give away leadership too soon.

18.   Do not delegate vision.

19.   Learn to lead though teams.

20.   Do not start a ministry without the right leadership in place.

21.   Learn to be an encourager.

22.   Do not be afraid to admit when you're wrong. Remember everything always come back to you and your leadership.

23.   Don't be afraid to take risks and big leaps of faith.

24.   Be who God made you to be, not someone else.

25.   Hold strong to your vision—it will be challenged.

Brian has a desire to leave a lasting impact on church planters. He sums up his desire in this final statement,

> My Legacy to church planters—I want to be remembered as a man that was faithful to my God and my family and consistent in my character, my friendships, and my walk with Christ. I want to be remembered as a man who truly loved and cared for others. I want to leave a legacy of big dreams and big faith. And I would like it to be said, that it was not about him; his life was lived to bring glory to God.

Soul

The passion of West Ridge Church is life change. Pastor Brian explains, "We want to see people get on a journey to become true, sold out, authentic Christ Followers."

They stay focused on this passion by addressing and creating four things in the lives of attendees and believers.

Love God through Worship: They are passionate about teaching people to love God with all their heart, soul, and mind. The focus is prayer, teaching, giving, fasting, corporate worship, and journaling.

Grow in God through Groups: They are passionate about relational ministry. The focus is small groups, Tuesday Night LIFEgroups, women's groups, single adult groups, men's groups, and age graded groups.

Serve God through Ministry Teams: They are passionate about their people using their spiritual gifts and finding their purpose in life. The focus is to have 80 percent of the student and adult population involved in serving on a ministry team.

Share God through Outreach: They are passionate about helping people engage their friends, their neighborhood, their community, their country, and the world with the love of Jesus Christ. The focus is to reach and invite, local community outreach, church planting, and cross-cultural missions.

Statistics and Structure

West Ridge Church has 52 full-time and part-time employees. They operate with a $5.2 million dollar budget, 18 percent of which is used for mission efforts. They have an average attendance above 4,000 and an Easter attendance in 2008 of more than 7,500. They have planted almost 30 churches with a total attendance of over 7,000 people each week. By 2010, they plan on having 50 church plants in operation.

The West Ridge campus occupies 62 acres with over 100,000 square feet of usable space.

The head of West Ridge Church is Jesus Christ. On a human level, three groups of people direct the ministries of West Ridge. Those bodies are the elders, the stewardship team, and the staff.

The *elders* are members of the body who provide general watch care and oversight. They evaluate the teaching ministry of the church, review major ministry decisions and strategic initiatives, and oversee church discipline. The lead pastor leads this team.

The *stewardship team* is made up of members of the church that are empowered by the elders to advise the elders and management team concerning the legal and financial aspects of the ministry and matters pertaining to buildings and facilities. They all have some marketplace expertise, which they use to serve the church.

Finally, the *staff* leads the day-to-day affairs of the sub ministries of the church. They are paid so that they can devote the best hours of their day to building ministries. The management team—a subgroup of the key leaders on staff, led by the lead pastor—directs the staff as a whole. The staff then supports the strategies and priorities determined by the management team. The main job of the staff is to build and coordinate teams of volunteers so that ministry can happen. The management team's main function is to give leadership to the staff and church.

The way the three groups work together can best be stated as follows: the staff directs and oversees the ministries of the church with overall leadership provided by the management team; these ministries are supported by the financial discernment and wisdom provided by the stewardship team; and all the activities of the church are carried out under the discernment and watch care of the elders.

What makes West Ridge work smoothly is the humble, servant like spirit of these groups of people. Leaders at all levels do not see it as their role to "lord it over" those in their charge, but desire to serve the body with their gifts and to build the kingdom rather than an "empire." Members of the church sense this servanthood in action and likewise esteem those in leadership. Whether as a leader or a follower, everyone in the church is submitted to Jesus Christ, and all consider others more important than themselves (Philippians 2:3). This spirit of cooperation and appreciation is one of God's greatest blessings to the body. It is a fragile gift, however, and any person desiring to become a member should value and protect it.

ABOUT THE CHURCH PLANTER—

Brian Bloye is founding and Lead Pastor of West Ridge Church (www. westridge.com), a Southern Baptist Church in Dallas, Georgia. The church's mission is "to lead people on a life-changing Journey to follow Jesus Christ." They practice four activities: Love, Grow, Serve, and Share.

Brian and his wife, Amy met in Lynchburg, Virginia, and they have served together in ministry since 1992.

Pastor Bloye is a 1988 graduate of Liberty University in Lynchburg (BS, communications), and earned a master of divinity degree (MDiv) in 1994 from Liberty Baptist Theological Seminary. He was ordained at Thomas Road Baptist Church in 1992.

He regularly writes a blog, www.brianbloye.org. Brian is the founder and President of Engage Atlanta, network of churches that have come together to transform Atlanta, and Net 35, a church planting network formed to plant prevailing churches all over the world.

Brian and Amy were married in 1992 and have two sons—John Taylor (1995) and Zachary (1998).

Chapter 9
A Church for All People

"Mosaic is a church that is breaking down ... barriers and changing our city's culture. (It's) influencing a systemic rethinking of things and setting an example that few churches to date have been willing to address."

- Mark Pryor (D–AR)
United States Senator

Story

Mark DeYmaz was raised in the Catholic faith. As an altar boy and a Jesuit high school student, he understood about having a religious life but not a *spiritual* life. In 1980, in the summer following his freshman year in college, Mark came to a saving faith in Christ Jesus through the college ministry of Scottsdale Baptist Church in Arizona.

That fall, Mark received a full athletic scholarship to play baseball at Liberty University. This began his journey in his newfound faith. As with many young students at Liberty, Mark was challenged with the ministry and message of Dr. Jerry Falwell. He states, "It was Dr. Falwell who first made me believe that I could be a Champion for Christ." Mark was inspired with the faith, courage, sacrifice, and desire for excellence taught and modeled in the life of Dr. Falwell.

Upon graduation from Liberty, Mark pursued that same excellence as a student ministries pastor serving in churches throughout Arizona, Oregon, Washington, and Germany. His ministries grew, and Mark became well known as an innovative and pioneering student ministries pastor.

In the spring of 1983, two churches invited Mark to lead their student ministries. One choice was a growing and diverse congregation in Seattle, Washington. The pastor was a former NFL linebacker and had built a strong ministry. Seattle was just two hours from Mark's wife Linda's hometown. He would be on the West Coast, have an opportunity to build the student ministry of his choice, and be near family.

The other choice was an equipping-oriented church located in Little Rock, Arkansas. This pastor had also built an incredible ministry in the southern landscapes of the United States. His inspiration and hospitality were emulated throughout the church. Mark's mother was born and raised in Arkansas—but there were some things that bothered this West Coast boy about coming to the South!

Seattle was a large city; Little Rock was not. Seattle was diverse in culture and ethnicity; Little Rock was not. Seattle was close to family; Little Rock was not. Seattle had a lot of rain; Little Rock had a lot of humidity. Seattle had Starbucks; Little Rock didn't. Seattle had any kind of food you would want; Little Rock did not—unless it was Southern.

Mark recalls a conversation with Linda as they were nearing the time to make a decision. He was thinking out loud and said,

> "I don't know, Linda. I like the fact that Antioch (Seattle) is a diverse church in a large city out west. I mean, after all, Little Rock is so much smaller than Seattle, and it's in the South—a long way from our families. Think about it! It's a city infamously associated with racism. In 1957, Central High School was forcibly integrated, and the schools are still controlled by the federal courts. Is this really where we want to raise our kids?"

> In response, Linda leaned her head around the corner and said, "But who knows, Mark? Maybe God will use you to change things."

"Yeah, right," I flippantly replied. "I'm not even from the South—an outsider—and I'm going to change several hundred years of racial prejudice and segregation?"[31]

The decision was made. In the summer of 1993, Mark and Linda moved their family to Little Rock, and God began to do a great work in the life of Fellowship Bible Church. In 1997, Mark was at the top of his game in student ministries. The youth were growing, and the ministry was healthy. Not only did they have numerical growth, but the Spirit was evident in their work. Mark also began meeting with other local church youth leaders and youth pastors. This meeting began to grow, and genuine relationships of friendship and trust were developed. There was only one problem, "one nagging reality: virtually the entire group was white."[32]

It was during this time that Mark sensed a stirring in his spirit about the "systemic segregation," both ethnic and economic, of his relationships in ministry and of his own church. He wondered why a town that was almost 40 percent African American would not be reflected in the ethnographic profile of his church. In fact, the only people of color were the church janitors.

In April of that year, Mark invited eight peer youth workers to meet for a morning of prayer and discussion. Of the group, four youth workers were white, and four were African American. After much discussion, it was determined that an event should be initiated that would gather youth workers and young people from each church, black or white, to declare that "Racism is, ultimately, a spiritual problem."[33]

On September 19, 1997, the Racial Reconciliation Rally was held at the River Market Amphitheatre in downtown Little Rock. This historic event brought together DC Talk, Billy Graham, Evander Holyfield, CeCe Wynans, Pastor E.V Hill, and Miles McPherson as well as local, state, and federal government officials and a large number of pastors, youth workers, and church members representing congregations of

---

31 *Building A Healthy Multi-Ethnic Church*, Mark DeYmaz, Jossey-Bass, 2007, page xx.
32 Ibid, page xxi.
33 Ibid, page xxii

various backgrounds and colors. The *Arkansas Democrat Gazette* quoted an African American pastor, "I believe the walls have come down."

This event increased the struggle in Mark's spirit. He was no longer content to "build a bridge to the community." He wanted to be a part of a church that was the community.[34]

In the fall of 2000, Mark decided it was time to see what God wanted to do with this ongoing discontent in his spirit. He prepared his résumé, made some calls, and waited—and then he met someone who would make a tremendous impression on his soul.

Precious Williams was an African American who grew up in Little Rock. She was a hairstylist at a local salon who was open to talk about her thoughts and feelings regarding the racial attitudes of the South. She liked having Mark as a customer. And during an Arkansas autumn, God used her to challenge his faith and change his life.

Mark recalls a specific day getting his hair cut by Precious. He writes in his book, *Building A Healthy Multi-Ethnic Church*,

> I remember sitting back in her chair one day and initially enjoying lighthearted conversation. At some point, however, we began talking about racism and, in particular, the segregation of the local church. I asked Precious if churches in Little Rock had always been segregated and what it was like for her, growing up in such a place. Had it affected her spiritually? Had it shaped her view of Christians, of the Church of God?
>
> Now I honestly do not recall all that she said in response, but I do remember what I asked her next. I said, "Precious, do you think there is a need in Little Rock for a diverse church, one where individuals of varying backgrounds might worship God together as one?"
>
> Her answer was no surprise.
>
> "Oh, yes, Mark," she said, in a quiet but hopeful tone.

---

34   Ibid, page xxiii

She went on to describe what she thought such a church might be like—what it would mean for the community—and to say that she, indeed, longed for the day.[35]

Mark relates the probing question that Precious asked — a question that would shake him to the very core of his being. She asked, "Mark, do you ever think it could happen here?"

He continues,

Now in the precise moment that Precious spoke these words to me, I experienced two remarkable things. Physically, I felt a very powerful rush of heat pass through my body—the same terrifying sensation you feel when someone scares you in the dark! Spiritually, however, something even more remarkable occurred.

For though I had heard with my ears—"Mark, do you ever think it could happen here?"—I simultaneously heard with my heart—"Mark, would you consider doing it here?"[36]

It was at that moment that Mark heard the call, similar to the call that Paul had received in Acts 16:9–10. Mark knew *Who* was calling and *what* he was called to do.

Not able to shake the excitement, he rushed home to tell Linda. Being confident of his calling and assured by the comments of Precious, he was certain Linda would be just as excited and ready to embrace the vision that God had revealed.

Her response was immediate. It was determined. It was definitive. It was no!

Linda had so looked forward to moving close to family, that any decision to remain in Little Rock and start a new church was too much to consider. She knew that Little Rock needed a diverse church. She

---

35   Ibid, page xxiv
36   Ibid, page xxiv

knew that God would bless this effort. She just wasn't convinced that her husband was the one called to undertake this overwhelming task.

Mark walked away knowing that he could never accomplish such a task without the full support of his wife. In the next few weeks, they continued to pray and seek God's confirmation. Faith was required, not only for the mission but for the first steps of beginning the ministry.

In the following weeks, Mark found his interest emerging as intention, his prayers evolving to pursuit. He began clarifying the need for such a ministry and his ability to be the man that God could use to build this ministry. The difficulty and sacrifice required was becoming a reality. Mark writes,

> Planting a church would be hard enough, but planting a multi-ethnic church would be even harder. Beyond that, to think that it could happen in Little Rock seemed outright impossible![37]

Mark again remembered the lessons that Jerry Falwell had lived, lessons of faith walking and trusting God. The sacrifice that would be required to trust God in accomplishing something only He could do was fleshed out in the ministry of Dr. Falwell and evidenced in the ministry of Liberty University and Thomas Road Baptist Church. Mark knew he could trust God and was reminded that "faith without works is dead" and that "without faith it is impossible to please God."

Although Mark knew that God had moved him, he still needed that additional assurance that God had called him, not his own desire to see a work born. He prayerfully and confidently asked God to lead him to peers and mentors who would confirm God's calling on his life—in 100 percent unanimity.

Without exception, each person had positive and instructive comments to Mark in starting a multi-ethnic church. They agreed that it was time and "long overdue." They agreed that the need was real. One well known and respected African American pastor told Mark

---

37   Ibid, page xxv

privately, "If anyone can do it, Mark, I believe you can. And if you do decide to go for it, you'll have my full support."[38]

Mark was overwhelmed; he was inspired; he was ready. He knew God was calling him and Linda to walk by faith and to trust God beyond their experience, beyond their education, beyond their ability, and beyond their understanding.

Mark sums it up by writing,

> So on May 17, 2001, Linda and I responded in prayer to a very specific call of God on our lives. That day, we committed ourselves and our family to a journey of faith, courage, and sacrifice that would lead to the establishment of a multi-ethnic and economically diverse church in the heart of Central Arkansas—a church formed in response to the prayer of Jesus Christ for unity and patterned after the New Testament church at Antioch (Acts 11:19 ff.)—a church for others, for all people, a church we called Mosaic.[39]

Strategy

Mosaic Church developed its purpose on a Scripture-based vision statement.

> Mosaic is a multi-ethnic and economically diverse church founded by men and women seeking to know God and to make Him known through the pursuit of unity, in accordance with the prayer of Jesus Christ (John 17:20–23) and patterned after the New Testament church at Antioch (Acts 11:19–26, 13:1 ff.).[40]

The primary purpose of Mosaic is to know God and to make Him known ... thus, the basis of unity. However, with such a diversity mandated from a visional practice, it was also necessary for this body to state what it is not.

38 Ibid, page xxv
39 Ibid, page xxvi
40 Ibid, page xxvi

> Mosaic is not a church focused on racial reconciliation.
> Rather, we are focused on reconciling men and women
> to God through Testament.[41]

These statements mandate the focus on Mosaic's two primary aspects of reconciliation. First, reconciling men and women to Jesus Christ through faith in His work of grace, and secondly, reconciling people to each other, also by faith through the work of His grace in lives as evidenced by the love shared among them. The group of believers in unison would pursue the New Testament principles and practices of loving God and loving others.

The reconciliation of men and women to God is likened to the work of evangelism. The reconciliation of men and women according to the principles and practices of the New Testament, evidenced by an obedient walk reflected in mutual love, is likened to the work of discipleship.

Evangelism and discipleship: these are the foundational elements of a biblically diverse New Testament church.

Mosaic was also established essentially on faith. Mark and Linda determined not to raise any funds before a decision had been reached to begin a ministry or program. This trust became the beginning steps of a faith walk that would be identified with the work of Mosaic Church. It was a decision that Mark and Linda shared—a decision that would be foundational to the core of their marriage.

Mark felt the decision to marry was also a walk of faith. Marriage requires that both husband and wife agree on the steps of faith that are necessary to build a ministry that only God can establish. Mark states, "The decision to marry is one that requires leaders to put families first with no regret, shame, or guilt."

Once they had determined that God had called them to Little Rock, they resigned their church with a three-month severance package and began praying that God would prompt people to support them in their new endeavor. It required great faith to trust Him, and God supplied more than was ever needed. Mark shares, "By September of 2001, we

41   Ibid, xxvii

were debt free and receiving more in monthly compensation than we ever had before! God had come through. God was with us. There could be no doubt."

Faith—trusting God with your future calling and trusting him with your daily needs—this, too, was a key strategy in Mosaic Church.

Location in building a multi-ethnic and diverse church was critical. In order to be a church for all people, it must be in an area where all people were located. In addition, it must be located where few boundaries kept people from attending.

It was important to locate in an area of need: not only where the church could meet social needs of people, but an area not already saturated by other churches or ministries. In the demographic analysis of this selected area, it was determined that more than 20 percent of the people living within the church's zip code lived at or below the poverty level. In addition, the area had the highest violent crime rate in the state.

This moved Mosaic to locate their church in the topographical center of Little Rock. This location would provide them with the greatest access to people and provide people with a common and familiar location. Mosaic also chose to "anchor" itself to an institution. They selected the University of Arkansas at Little Rock.

Location: situated where the people are and where the needs are most evident.

Faith-walking: satisfied with a trust and faith in God, depending on Him to build His church.

Reconciliation: of men and women to God, and of people to each other through the principles and practices of God's Word. This is seen in the evangelism of the lost and discipleship of believers.

As these strategies were put into practice, fruit of the labor was revealing. Mark writes,

> In our case, such understanding led to the conversion
> of some forty-three individual within the first eighteen

months of Mosaic (July 2001 to January 2003). This included men and women from seven different nations in a city where internationals have come to dwell in increasingly significant numbers.

Amazingly, our first convert was a 32-year-old Muslim man from Saudi Arabia just three months after the horrific 9/11 attacks. The public testimony of faith he shared at the church just three weeks following his conversion led that same evening to the salvation of a university student from Japan and, in the days following, to the conversion of a 24-year-old Australian woman, as well as a man from Mexico in his mid-forties.[42]

Successes

The greatest success credited to Mosaic Church is the attainment of their vision statement. Their unique theology and ecclesiology of a multi-ethnic diverse church has become a new beacon of hope to the segregated congregations that consume the landscape of America's churches. As stated before, Mosaic is not a church that focuses solely on racial reconciliation, but on the reconciliation of men and women to God through faith in Jesus Christ and on mutual reconciliation as a congregation through the principles and practices of the first century church as seen in Antioch and Ephesus.[43]

It is Mosaic's desire to have a place where men and women, black and white, multi-ethnicity and economic diversity would find a common place where they could walk, work, and worship God together as one. This concept has become the chorus of this church with its emerging global influence for the cause of Christ.

Struggles

As in any church plant, identifying, instructing, and implementing leadership at all levels is critical.

---

42   Ibid, page xxviii
43   *Church Planting Summary Report* submitted by Mark DeYmaz; Bob Miller, 2008, page 4

Mosaic showed success at various levels of leadership development, but was lacking in the area of developing elders. Mark understood *identifying* the qualifications of elders and deacons as listed in 1 Timothy 3 and Titus 3. However, they soon learned that these were the minimal standards for leadership. The initial vetting of a potential servant leader or shepherd must consider more than just the spiritual and initial character issues. Additional consideration of skill set, gift mix, role preference, team fit, experience, capacity, and capability must all be considered in evaluating and selecting leadership for the church.

Instructing potential church leadership made it necessary for Mosaic not only to have the standards and qualifications in writing for potential candidates, but also to present the vision and mission of the church and have them embraced. When one talks of building a "multi-ethnic and diverse" church, the images of how that is implemented varies from person to person. It becomes necessary to have some type of written proposal that clearly articulates and defines the vision of the church and its leaders and spells out its mission. Write the vision and mission early on, and use it as a teaching tool to potential leaders.

Implementing church leadership also needs to be a consideration for leadership development. Mosaic recommends an elder's handbook or guide that details the roles and expectations of those who become servant leaders. Detailed procedures, biblically based, on making decisions, handling conflict, and leading the flock will prepare and sustain leadership. Mark encourages pastors, "Before appointing men to the office, walk them through this document, and have them sign off in agreement."[44]

Significance

The mission of Mosaic Church is reviving faith, restoring hope, and revealing love. Through the Mosaic Church of Central Arkansas, black, brown, yellow, and white Americans, representing more than thirty nations, have come together as one.

Professionals, white-collar workers, the working middle class, and those with limited means have found a home in this unique church for

44   Ibid, page 5

all people. The result of their combined work, efforts, and compassion for each other has created a significant ministry.

Hungry people are being fed. The homeless are being clothed. Prisoners are being visited. The sick are being healed. Communities are being developed. Faith is being revived, hope restored, and love revealed.

Mark writes,

> According to research conducted at the turn of the century by sociologists Curtiss Paul Deyoung, Michael O. Emerson, George Yancey, and Karen Chai Kim, 92.5 percent of Catholic and Protestant churches throughout the United States can be classified as "monoracial."

> This term describes a church in which 80 percent or more of the individuals who attend are of the same ethnicity or race. The remaining churches (7.5 percent) can be described as multiracial—churches in which there are a non-majority, collective population of at least 20 percent. By this definition approximately 12 percent of Catholic churches, just less than 5 percent of Evangelical churches, and about *2.5 percent of mainline Protestant churches can be described as multiracial.*[45]

Soul

Multi-ethnic and economic diversity are practiced so that the world might know God's grace, witness His love, and experience the church's belief (John 17:20–23). Mosaic is a place where diverse individuals from varying backgrounds walk, work, and worship God together, as one, reflecting the kingdom of God on earth as it is in heaven.[46]

Mosaic describes itself as a church focused on the needs of others and on reviving faith in others who feel disconnected from care and concern.

---

45   Ibid, page 5
46   *Church Planting Summary Report* submitted by Mark DeYmaz; Bob Miller, 2008, page 6

Mosaic is a place free of distinction.

Mosaic is a place where a homeless man may be warmly embraced and helped with rehab; he has been sober for three years and now holds a steady job.

Mosaic is a place where a woman finds healing from the wounds of a father who abandoned her as a child.

Mosaic is a place where one turns to God after being physically abused by her husband. She now has hope and prays for him.

Mosaic is a place where food and clothing are distributed twice a week to people in need.

Mosaic is a place where tutoring is also provided for Latino young people.

And Mosaic is a place where the church provides immigration counseling and legal services.

The soul of the church is evident in the souls of the people. Some of their stories ...

Raymond

Not long after Mosaic had moved into the old Wal-Mart, a homeless man named Raymond began attending faithfully from week to week. Typical of those on the street, he was disheveled and, in his case, often reeking of alcohol. Each Sunday, he would first head for the bathroom to clean himself up before coming back to get a cup of coffee and sit down for worship.

One morning during the service, I invited the congregation to break up into smaller groups for prayer. As I left the platform, a young high school girl named Sandra motioned to me. She was concerned for Raymond, who was sitting close to her, and wanted me to pray with him. Sitting down with the man, I began to talk with him and, more importantly, to listen.

During our brief exchange, Raymond spoke sincerely from his heart. He confessed that drugs and alcohol had consumed his life and had left him isolated from family members living nearby. At Mosaic, he said, the people were friendly and treated him kindly. Coming to Mosaic each week gave him peace and hope. He said, "I feel so good here! I feel the Spirit of God here. I may live like hell Monday through Saturday, but I like to come here on Sunday because it makes me feel so damn good!"

Taking hold of his hands, I prayed for him and, touched by his interaction, concluded the prayer time by asking Raymond to come forward to share his story with the rest of the body. As he spoke, it was evident to all that Raymond truly desired to be cleansed from his addictions and restored to his family. Having shared from his brokenness and of his despair, Raymond asked the church to come and pray for him.

In response, about a dozen Mosaics came forward and embraced him warmly.

It was the first physical touch or affection he had received in a very long time. Laying their hands upon him, they led the entire church in praying for Raymond that day. It was a beautiful sight to see; the body of Christ extending the love of God to this man who had come "just as I am." There wasn't a dry eye in the house.

Not long after this, two men from Mosaic helped Raymond to enroll in a 28-day detoxification program. He then entered rehabilitation and, after completing it, came by the church a completely different man. Soon Raymond, again, stood before the church; this time to ask forgiveness for the times he had taken advantage of generosity. More importantly, he shared that he had recently committed his life to Christ![1]

Ofelia Lima

Lori Tarpley, a member of Mosaic, works for the Myeloma Institute for Research and Therapy (MIRT) at the University of Arkansas for Medical Sciences (UAMS) in Little Rock. MIRT is focused on treating patients from around the world with multiple myeloma, a type of cancer related to lymphoma and leukemia. In time, those diagnosed with the disease become crippled and, sometimes, even paralyzed. There is no known cure.

In the spring of 2005, Lori was introduced at MIRT to a 72-year old woman from Cuba named Ofelia Lima and her daughter, Lissette. According to Lori, "It was clear that these folks were pretty lost; empty emotionally and at the end of the road. Ms. Lima had had myeloma for more than two years, and doctors in Miami had told her there was nothing more that could be done.

"'This disease,' they said, 'will take your life.'" Lissette learned about MIRT and decided that, before they gave up completely, she would bring her mother to Little Rock.

As an intake specialist, Lori did not usually invite patients to church. "But somehow," she said "in that initial interview, it was clear to me that I should take a chance and invite Ms. Lima to connect with our Latino community at Mosaic. I knew that our folks would be supportive."

From here, Ms. Lima picks up the story:

"From the moment I first entered Mosaic, I could sense something telling me, 'You are going to be healed. You do not have anything, you do not have cancer.' I bowed my head and prayed … and the brothers and sisters at Mosaic prayed for me, too. I heard a voice telling me,

'Everything is going to be fine.' And I left that place crying."

The very next day, Ms. Lima returned to MIRT in order to get the results of tests taken the week before. An MRI (magnetic resonance imaging) confirmed well over 100 holes and lesions where the myeloma had done its damage. As Lori read a second test to determine what disease was active, however, she was amazed: The test showed absolutely no active myeloma in Ms. Lima!

"That's not normal," said Lori. "One hundred lesions don't just empty out over the course of a weekend. It was clearly the fingerprint of God."

Ms. Lima and Lissette soon returned to Miami, healed in every way. And on her final Sunday at Mosaic, she stood for the first time in nine months, pushing aside the wheelchair to which she had been bound. "In Little Rock," she said, "I was filled with joy, inside and out. It was here I began to walk again … and God is who I walk for."

Having been told she would be in Little Rock to undergo intense treatment of her disease for six months, Ms. Lima returned with Lissette to Miami after only twelve days! As of January 2007, Ms. Lima continues to do well. There remains no evidence of the disease.[47]

Georgia Mjarten

Georgia Mjartan is the Executive Director of Our House, a shelter in Little Rock that provides the working homeless with safe housing, food, child care, education, and job training.

---

47   Ibid

Her story speaks to the compelling nature and power of unity:

"I visited Mosaic for the first time on January 14, 2007, and on that day, Christ came into my heart. Before then, my concept of 'God' was very abstract and removed from day-to-day life. When people referred to God as someone who was working in their lives, I thought they were being disingenuous.

"In the summer of 2006, a man named Corey Ford came into the shelter. Corey was 6'2" and tattooed up and down his arms and neck. A former drug addict, he spent four and a half years in prison. Yet he was working in my shelter and truly concerned about the welfare of those around him. When Corey told me how God was working in his life, I believed him. How else, but by the power of God, could someone be so truly transformed?

"In January, Corey invited me to attend his church, Mosaic. On that Sunday, we arrived early and just in time for the weekly prayer meeting. Sitting with others in a small circle of prayer, I felt God's presence. Here were people of all different backgrounds, whose prayers sounded different—different intonation, different words—and all of these people were praying together to one God. Somehow I knew that God could hear these prayers. I did not have a question about that anymore.

"As the room filled, I felt overwhelmed with joy. There were black people and white people, Hispanic people, deaf people, Asians, families with babies, and the blind. We were young and old, students and professionals, wealthy and poor. I felt at home in this place and with these people. I felt God's presence in the music, in our connectedness, and in our prayers.

"During the service, there was also a time of communion. Whenever I had witnessed communion as a visitor in other churches prior to this, I had always stayed in my seat. I knew what communion represented, and I knew that participation meant personally accepting Christ's sacrifice. However, when communion began at Mosaic, I knew I was now ready to take part. In that moment I chose Christ, accepting Him and His sacrifice for me.

"After communion, there was worship and praise. I closed my eyes. I told myself that it wouldn't matter what anyone else thought of me. This was between me and my God. As I began to worship, I felt Christ's glory all around me. My hands lifted up to Him. Christ had come into my heart, and He is now a part of my day-to-day life!"[48]

Summary

It began as a simple children's song that we learned growing up in the church,

> *"Jesus loves the little children,*
> *all the children of the world.*
> *Red and yellow, black and white,*
> *they are precious in His sight.*
> *Jesus loves the little children of the world."*

Although the truth is evident through this simple children's song, its reach goes far beyond that. Mark DeYmaz and Mosaic have challenged each to look beyond the racism and racial reconciliation and see the redemptive relationships and works that are established through God's Word and with His character.

Mark summarizes his thoughts and challenge to young church planters:

Failure on the part of Christian leaders, then, to recognize the changing demographic landscape or

---

48   Ibid

to adapt—both personally and corporately—in accordance with Scripture will soon render their work or, worse yet, their message irrelevant.

There are already signs that increasing numbers of people are no longer finding credible the message that God loves all people as preached from segregated pulpits and pews.

Indeed, those without Christ are no longer responding simply to the words of our lips; rather, they will respond only to the love of God they see in us; love that is daily displayed in a genuine, personal love for all people in His name.

And this is best manifest in and through the establishment of healthy multi-ethnic local churches whereby believers of diverse ethnic and economic background can build cross-cultural relationships, pursue cross-cultural competency, promote a spirit of inclusion, and mobilize for impact as one people group.[49]

Statistics and Structure

As of December 2008, Mosaic offers three Sunday services in one venue with 600–650 people attending each week. The church consists of men and women from 30 nations, in an environment where no more than 50 percent of its membership is white. Only 2-3 percent of all churches through the United States have such diversity.

For nearly five years, the church met in an abandoned Wal-Mart before purchasing an old K-Mart store for $2 million in its target area. The facility provides 100,000 square feet of space on ten acres occupying one of the three busiest intersections in the state of Arkansas.[50]

---

49   Ibid, page 6
50   Ibid

Currently, the church operates on a budget of approximately $650,000 a year. There are ten people who receive some form of compensation.

Mosaic is an elder-led congregation. It is also multi-ethnic and diverse in its economic culture. It has a team teaching approach, with three teaching pastors rotating and sharing the pulpit. The music styles and content varies from week to week, reflecting the diversity of the congregation.

In addition, Mosaic is part of the Mosaix Global Network. Mosaix Global Network represents a growing movement of believers and congregations seeking to know God and to make Him known through the establishment of multi-ethnic churches throughout North America and beyond.

Founded in 2004 by Dr. Mark DeYmaz and Dr. George Yancey, the network exists to catalyze the growing movement toward multi-ethnic churches throughout North America and beyond by (1) casting vision, (2) connecting individuals and churches of like mind, (3) conferencing, and (4) coaching.[51]

"The Faith Community is essential in our efforts to dismantle racism; (and) Mosaic Church, in but a few short years, is already serving as a model for how a church can ... celebrate the richness of diversity."

- Jim Dailey, Former Mayor of Little Rock

ABOUT THE CHURCH PLANTER—

Dr. Mark DeYmaz is the founding Pastor and directional leader of the Mosaic Church of Central Arkansas (www.mosaicchurch.net), a multi-ethnic and economically diverse church in Little Rock, where significant percentages of black and white Americans, together with men and women from more than thirty nations, walk, work and worship God together as one.

A recognized leader in the emerging Multi-ethnic Church Movement, through his book, *Building a Healthy Multi-ethnic Church* (Jossey-Bass/

---

51   www.mosaicchurch.net, Affiliations page

Leadership Network, 2007), he provides the biblical mandate for the multi-ethnic church and outlines seven core commitments required to bring it about.

He posts weekly on his blog, *Glue,* at www.markdeymaz.com and is a contributing editor for *Leadership Journal.*

Mark is a graduate of Liberty University in Lynchburg, Virginia (B.S., Psychology), Western Seminary in Portland, Oregon (M.A., Exegetical Theology) and Phoenix Seminary in Phoenix, Arizona (D. Min.). He was ordained at Central Bible Church in Portland, Oregon, in 1987.

Married since 1987, Mark and Linda have four children—Zack, Emily, Will, and Kate.

Chapter 10
Multisite & Creative Strategies

*"Our biggest mistake when starting our first campus was that
we overlooked the validity and viciousness of spiritual warfare.
We learned the hard way that the enemy attacks God's plans in
their infancy stages. ... When God sent Moses to deliver Israel,
Pharaoh killed all the babies. When God sent Jesus to save the
world, Herod killed all the babies. Satan attacks ministries when
they are 'babies' because they are most vulnerable in their infancy.
We simply were not prepared at Discovery for spiritual warfare."*

-   Randy Smith

I first met Randy Smith in 1977 on Treasure Island, a youth camp in
Lynchburg, Virginia, set in the middle of the James River. I was from
Florida; he was from New Jersey. We both wanted to work with young
people, both had a heart for ministry, both type A personalities—and
at one point, both dated the same girl. We both traveled for Youth
Aflame Singers in the late 1970s, and that's where I learned to appreciate
Randy's love for life, his love for God, and his love for people.

I will always remember a trip that Randy and I took to St. Petersburg,
Florida, to work as an advance team for Youth Aflame. We went ahead
to set up church concerts and high school assemblies. During our prep
trip, we visited a radio station. We told the station manager that we
were from Liberty Baptist College and that Dr. Jerry Falwell had sent
us to this area of Florida to promote one of the College's singing teams;
we were stretching the truth just a bit. We asked if we could record a
radio intro that would air before Dr. Falwell's daily program. Within
minutes, he had us set up in front of a microphone and gave us the
go-ahead. Neither Randy nor had I ever done any recording like this

before. We quickly wrote a script, recorded the message (in less than five takes), and gave instructions to the radio station manager on when to run the announcement. We got back in the car, laughing and scared at the same time. On that day, I found a lifetime friend—or accomplice.

Randy has been involved in ministry for over 25 years.

While a student at Liberty University, Randy was a team leader for the Youth Aflame Singers, traveling throughout the United States and ten foreign countries performing "To People With Love" in high schools, amusement parks, malls, and churches. After graduation Randy ministered in St. Petersburg, Florida, where he was ordained at a Southern Baptist church. He later co-founded Calvary Chapel of St. Petersburg and Single Purpose, an area-wide single adult ministry.

In June of 1984, Randy moved back to New Jersey where he worked in a local church for 18 years as an outreach pastor. During that time he wrote and directed some of the Delaware Valley's largest Christmas and Easter productions and introduced the use of drama, video, media, and the creative arts into local church weekend services.

In 2003, Randy founded Discovery Church with the goal of using a balance of the arts and anointed teaching to reach "every person, in any way possible, today."

Story

The first regular service of Discovery Church was held on January 20, 2003, in the gym of the Voorhees Middle School in Voorhees, New Jersey. The core of initial leaders had grown up in church, worked in church, and basically devoted their lives to church—yet they were seeking more.

The young and restless group used to meet during the previous year at local diners or restaurants and talk "church" over multiple cups of coffee. They had visions of a *balanced* ministry and were *obsessed* with reaching the unchurched. They were *consumed* with teaching believers how to be fully devoted followers of Christ. They also wanted to attract seekers as well as thrill and teach believers with the truths of

Scripture. Additionally, they wanted to use a balance of the arts and anointed teaching to craft services and ministries that were relevant, enthusiastic, and cutting edge. They believed it was a sin for church to be boring!

After many late night conversations, these church planters determined that they wanted to see God's principles in control. They wanted to work as a team to cultivate fully devoted followers of Jesus Christ, who were growing spiritually, experiencing community, and using their spiritual gifts and resources to propel the ministry into the whole world. In other words, there would be a proper balance of "grace, growth, groups, gifts, and good stewardship." They wanted to do church in a new way, and these would be the measurements used to gauge the success of their ministry and influence.

The late-night coffee group had visions of developing a powerful evangelistic army that would work together to win their communities as they walked with God. That God-given vision of balanced ministry, along with scriptural principles, formed the foundation of Discovery Church's balanced approach.

After a year of talking, dreaming and praying about what a church should be, Randy and his team realized it was time for dreams to move out from behind the tables of PJ's, TGI Friday's, and the P&B Diner.

In 2003, Discovery Church began to realize the dream to reach out to the population of the Delaware Valley through an innovative approach involving the use of contemporary music, performing arts, and multimedia to communicate practical messages from the Bible. A second campus was opened in Washington Township in 2005, and a third campus was opened in Woolwich Township in 2008. A fourth campus—a college church—launches in the spring of 2009.

Discovery Church is interdenominational, adheres to a unique philosophy of working together as a team to present a balanced ministry, and offers weekend services and home fellowships called LIFEgroups.

In the weekend services, the performing arts, multimedia, upbeat music, and relevant teaching are used to present the timeless truths of

Scripture in ways that make sense even to someone who has never been in church before.

The relaxed dress code of Discovery is different than most churches. On any given day you'll see people wearing everything from golf shirts to pantsuits, sport coats to jeans, and even shorts in the summer. Basically, attendees are encouraged to wear what they are comfortable in.

Though nontraditional in style, Discovery is deeply committed to the eternal truths of the Christian faith. Their vision is simple: *to become a biblically functioning community of believers so that Christ's redemptive purposes can be accomplished in this world.* Their mission is equally clear: *to work together to turn irreligious people into fully devoted followers of Jesus Christ.*

Strategy

There were several keys to the strategy of launching Discovery.

The foundational strategy is *prayer.* One of the first things Randy realized about church planting was his need to "get on his knees and fight like a man." Randy writes,

> It's the Lord who builds His church. Our part is to pray, listen to what He says, and then do it. We built Discovery on the foundation of prayer long before our first service. We recruited everyone we know to pray for us. From the birth of the idea to the launch of the church and to this day, prayer was and is a central part of what we do at Discovery.

Another key strategy is *launching large.* A key aspect of planting purpose-driven churches is to begin large. The goal is to gather a crowd and turn the crowd into a church. Tommy Barnett says, "Without vision, people perish. Without people, the vision perishes." *Launching large brings in people.*

In his book, *The Purpose-Driven Church*, Rick Warren writes,

I've noticed over and over that if a church doesn't get beyond 200 within about a year and a half, it usually doesn't happen at all. On the other hand, churches that get over 200 in the first year just keep on growing and growing.

The goal of launching large is to get to a crowd right from the beginning and move forward from there.

According to NEXT Church Planting (<u>www. nextinitiative.net</u>), a large launch brings several distinct benefits to a church:

1. It breaks growth barriers. The best way to break growth barriers is quickly!

2. It brings credibility.

3. It provides a larger group of people to assimilate.

4. It facilitates self-support faster.

5. It creates excitement and enthusiasm.

Randy continues to comment,

Additionally, when you launch with a once-a-month "Preview Service," you have more time between previews to connect with visitors and new Christ-followers. Preview services are like previews for an upcoming movie. Previews begin with several once-a-month services and end with a grand opening service followed by week-to-week services. Preview services introduce the community to what the church will be like, and the staff meetings in between previews give the church planting team the time needed to evaluate and do the job well.

However, according to NEXT, there is a price for launching large. The added stress, the higher costs of marketing and equipment, as well as the advance preparation needed make launching large more difficult than other church planting models. There is also rapid change in this model, so the planter must be willing to adjust.

Randy writes on the impact of these strategies:

> Overall, the prayer and planning combined with the Preview Service and launching large format combined to give each of our campuses first week attendances of over 140 people.

Discovery Church has also initiated a multisite strategy. Randy comments,

> One of the motivating goals of Discovery Church is to plant forty local churches in twenty years. While there are many ways to accomplish this task, we believe God's called us to be a multisite organization when it comes to planting churches in the Delaware Valley. Simply put, we think the best way to start and grow new churches is to plant a number of "hub" sites that will each then "spider-web" out across the Delaware Valley in 15-mile steps called "campuses." Each new campus will grow and mature as well as work with the existing campuses to train the people and provide the resources needed to start even more churches.

Randy feels the criteria for starting new sites are based on attendees coming from the same area that is over fifteen to twenty miles from the current location. When there is a core of "distance attendees," and they are able to sustain a significant infrastructure, they will begin the process of developing a new site.

This technique is commonly called the "multi-site church planting process," and it is a phenomenon that you will no doubt be hearing about in the future. An estimated 2,000 churches nationwide are experimenting with this concept: one church (meaning one staff, one leadership team, one budget) meeting in multiple locations, with the various sites developing unique personalities yet sharing the same "brand identity" and DNA.

The benefits of a multi-site strategy are numerous, but the most important are these: (1) the church is not built on any one person, and (2) since the sites are smaller than one "mega-church" (200–300 people per site), it is easier not to get lost in the crowd. On the other hand, sharing budgets and staff means the resources are comparable to those of a mega-church (enabling more ministry), and people are doing the jobs God designed and gifted them to do. In short, ministry is increased.

Randy shares how a multi-site strategy works for Discovery:

> There is one staff, one leadership team, and one budget for a certain number of sites in one geographical area. Each of these geographical areas will have four to six campuses. The campuses share resources and support ministries while teaching pastors and worship teams rotate between locations. Each campus has a campus pastor who serves as the "face with the place." The campus pastor hosts the large group events and weekend services at the church campus; assists with the administration of discipleship, equipping ministries, and small group ministries for that campus; and serves as the liaison to the larger community in which the facility is located.

Randy continues,

> For example, in our current situation, Bob Smith is the campus pastor at Voorhees, while Josh Hathaway is the campus pastor at the Washington Township campus. These guys are on site every Sunday, and each oversees a specific location. While one of the teaching pastors teaches a three-week series in Voorhees, Randy (another teaching pastor) does the same in Washington Township, or in Woolwich, or at ETHOS college church. Then they switch. During the week, all the locations come together at a central location (the "hub") for church administration, combined campus student ministry, the ladies ministry, music practice,

leadership training, or a worship and praise night. Of course, two keys to this strategy are LIFEgroups and a good administrative team at each campus. Eventually we want to see forty of these campuses established in the next twenty years.

Successes

Randy credits the success of Discovery to the launching large strategy, as well as the success of recruiting teams consisting of leadership and volunteers. He shares,

> Teamwork makes the dream work! Our strategy for doing so is simple. First, we starting praying as a staff and as a church for God to supply the co-workers we need. Each piece of equipment we need (and its price) as well as each of the key positions we need to lead the essential teams is listed in a monthly prayer newsletter. This not only gives people specifics to pray about, it can be used to help people see where they can give or be used.

Sharing the vision is also a key to the ministry success of Discovery. Randy says,

> We also begin to share the strategy and vision for that new campus with as many people as possible. This is done in sermons, videos sent to LIFEgroups, newsletters, programs (bulletins), podcasts, and even on Facebook and by Twitter.

Staff members are also instructed to identify and talk to likely leaders. These potential team members will receive training and then could recruit and lead their own teams. The staff of Discovery will share the vision with these potential leaders and ask for their help. Randy explains,

> We tell them what we need ... listing the specific ministry ... and tell them why we believe God can use

them in this ministry. Most importantly, we don't ask them to just pray generally about it. We challenge them to ask God if He is in this. Finally, we set a date of about one week to follow up for their reply.

Ron Sylvia, author of *Starting New Churches on Purpose*, says it best: "God is not mute and He can communicate with them in a week's time!"

Once new leaders and team members are recruited, the Discovery staff trains and continually coaches them. Each team member is encouraged to read *Starting New Churches on Purpose*. The staff also hosts training meetings with teaching DVDs from leading church planting organizations and takes leadership recruits to conferences to interact with other leadership teams from like-minded churches. These team members are the nucleus of each new campus.

Randy talks about the greatest key to success: "First, we *enable* or train them to do the job, then we *empower* them with the decision making tools to do so. We let our leaders lead. We do NOT lead by committee!"

Struggles

One of the greatest struggles that Randy and Discovery Church has faced is spiritual warfare. Randy writes,

> John Maxwell's books have encouraged me to "fail forward" by learning from my mistakes. Our biggest mistake when starting our first campus was that we overlooked the validity and viciousness of spiritual warfare. We learned the hard way that the enemy attacks God's plans in their infancy stages. You can see this truth illustrated throughout Scripture. When God sent Moses to deliver Israel, Pharaoh killed all the babies. When God sent Jesus to save the world, Herod killed all the babies. Satan attacks ministries when they are "babies" because they are most vulnerable in their

infancy. We simply were not prepared at Discovery for spiritual warfare.

Randy concludes,

We now pray and do spiritual warfare before even starting the plans for a new campus. We have learned that prayer and spiritual warfare must be priorities, and when they are, Satan cowers in fear.

Significance

One of the most unique characteristics of Discovery Church is their use of the creative arts in their regular worship experiences. Randy comments on the use of creativity,

The one thing that makes Discovery stand out in the crowd of new church plants is our creativity. Our mantra is "It is a sin to be boring!" and we strive to make each Sunday Experience (service) a place where God's Word is creatively taught and shared. Most of that creativity comes from our amazing creative team and the specific procedure they follow for creativity.

The emphasis is not just on the worship experience, but also in the planning strategies that occur for each service. Randy explains "a very unique and shared process":

First of all, all of our sermon and creative planning is done as a team. This is a HUGE paradigm shift for most pastors. In most churches, worship planning usually involves just two people—the senior pastor and the worship pastor. The senior pastor simply tells the worship pastor what the sermon is going to be about for the weekend. This usually takes place around Thursday! Then the worship pastor might select songs accordingly, and if the message and music worked together, it was a work of God.

Randy goes on to explain the benefits that Discovery has seen from planning as a team.

First, you get *Better Content:* Teaching is better the more input it has.

> *Better Creativity* is another result. It's time we admit it—solo preaching has become a creativity bottleneck in the local church. One person can only be creative for so long before they stagnate. Creativity and planning happens best in numbers.
>
> The third result is *Better Context:* More people involved in the process results in more stories and illustrations!
>
> Finally, planning as a team results in *Better Control of Your Time:* You will get a better message in less time, have more time to plan and prepare, AND have better messages all the time! At Discovery, we plan message series up to twelve weeks ahead of time with a team of people.
>
> The secret of creativity is to tap into the reservoir of creativity of the people God brings to each of us. Learning how to do that is one reason Discovery is so creative.

Randy shares a few secrets to having a creative meeting.

> First, we invite creative people to a meeting NOT to be on the creative team. If we discover they are not creative or don't have the right chemistry, we simply do not invite them back. It is easier not to invite them to another meeting than to remove them from a team.
>
> Second, we come to the creative meetings prepared. We e-mail the topic, simple outline, and relevant verses to the team members about a week before. When the

entire team has a chance to research before the meeting, it makes for a highly productive meeting.

Third, the goal of a creative meeting is to brainstorm on how to introduce creative elements into every aspect of the worship service—from the moment the crowd arrives to the moment they drive away. Creative elements should create emotional and spiritual responses, stimulate thinking, and cause the listener to do (or write) something. In the creative process we ask ourselves, *"How can we incorporate sight, sound, smell, taste, touch into the worship experience?"*

Creative elements can be video clips, message video roll-ins, dramas, My Stories (testimonies), video or live interviews, dance, or a powerful song. We vary the types of elements throughout the series to keep the service from becoming too predictable.

When it's all said and done, we want people to say they met God in a special way at Discovery. We want them to say, *"Wow! That was church?"*

Summary

Randy wrote the following in the new NEXT Church Planting curriculum published by LifeWay:

Make no mistake about it, while church planting is in vogue today, it is still not as effective as it should be. Our prayer is that your church will break the pattern. Understand, it costs more than ever to launch a church, financially and emotionally. But also understand this— the cost is worth it. You'll understand that when the first person in your new church accepts Christ as their Lord, Leader, and Forgiver. It is worth it all!

Soul

The soul of Discovery can be found in its mission statement: "To work together as a team to turn irreligious people into fully devoted Christ-followers." Its goal is to be used by God to change lives, and its soul is to do so as a team.

Discovery members firmly believe that teamwork is a strategy for building the church. In sync, they promote the "teamwork strategy" as the way to work together and introduce people to Christ. It is the way they "reach everyone, in any way possible, today!" It also guides them to maturity in Christ. In short, the "teamwork strategy" is the track Discovery follows together to cultivate fully devoted followers of Christ.

Here is the "teamwork strategy" as taught in Discovery's new member's class:

> *T – "Take the time" – Invest in someone" – Make a Connection*
>
> Rather than just beginning with the message of Christ, we seek to make connections so that when we do share the message, we have credibility. You need to have relationships with a reason! In short, you have to invest in people before you can invite them!
>
> *E – "Explain your story" – Introduce them to your story – Share a Verbal Witness*
>
> It is not enough just to be "nice people"—unbelievers must eventually hear why we are the way we are, Who can save them, and how.
>
> *A – "Ask them to church" - Invite them to a Weekend Service*
>
> Discovery's "weekend service" is designed to supplement the evangelistic efforts made on the part of the believer to reach the nonbeliever. Every weekend, we use the weekend services at the church to present some facet

of the message of Christ—our goal is to give people Jesus—the answer to life in the 21st century.

Discovery also hosts praise and worship nights so believers can experience worship through song and prayer.

M – "Move to 411" – Grow spiritually through discipleship

Our 411 Discipleship Groups (four people who meet one hour a week for one purpose—spiritual growth) are a great way to get grounded in the basics of the faith.

W – "Walk with God" – Grow spiritually individually

It is critical that new believers grow and mature in the faith. Developing the ability to read God's Word, pray, worship, and sense God's leading are all part of the spiritual growth process.

O – "Open Up in small groups" – Grow spiritually in a small group

Life change happens best when a small group of believers gather to share their lives, learn from God's Word in a discussion format, and serve one another.

R – "Recognize & use your gifts" – Serve in the Body of Christ

K – "Keep God first in your time, talent & treasure" – Steward your resources & serve

When God becomes master of our time, our talents and our treasure (our spending and giving habits), we can be reasonably confident He is master over all the areas of our lives.

Statistics and Structure

Discovery averages 200–300 attendees per site. Paid staff positions vary from a part-time children's director at each site to a children's pastor and campus pastors at each site (who also have other responsibilities such as student pastor, etc.). They have several administrative assistants, three part-time teaching pastors, a part-time LIFEgroups pastor who attends seminary, a full-time creative arts pastor, and a lead pastor.

Offerings average out to about $18–20 per attendee (lower than the national average giving of $23 per person). Discovery had no support and was not a part of any denomination when they planted. They are considering affiliation with the Southern Baptists.

Discovery is a "staff-led, team-run" church. Staff members oversee all matters of the church and its operations as long as such decisions stay within the boundaries of a predetermined and approved vision, mission, and core values. They have lay leaders who oversee the finances of Discovery, and others are available for consultation. Ultimately the staff oversees the operations of the church. The lead pastor is the head of the staff and church, and the management team leads with him.

The most important leadership groups are the various ministry teams. Discovery believes that every member should have a vital place in strategic service on a ministry team. As part of a team, all players are valuable, and their input is significant. Those are the people who make Discovery work.

ABOUT THE CHURCH PLANTER—

Randy Smith is founding and Lead Pastor of Discovery Church in Washington Township, New Jersey (www.discoverychurchnj.com), an independent, non-denominational church.

Randy is a 1980 graduate of Liberty University in Lynchburg, Virginia (B.S., Religion) and is currently pursuing a M.A. in Church Planting from Liberty Theological Seminary. He was ordained at Northside Baptist Church, St. Petersburg, Florida, 1982.

He regularly writes a blog, www.randyRsmith.com. Randy is a regular featured speaker at the national and regional Purpose Driven Church Planting Conferences, has served monthly as a Purpose Driven Church Planting Coach at Saddleback Church and other churches and has taught at the following conferences: Willow Creek Arts Conference, the Purpose Driven Church Conference, and the Purpose Driven Worship Conference.

Randy and his wife Karen grew up in New Jersey and have worked together in business and served together in ministry since 1986. Randy and Karen were married in 1986 and have one daughter, Camryn (2002).

Chapter 11
One Church—Many Locations

*"Worth more than the support that Liberty Baptist Fellowship
was giving us was what Dr. Falwell did before we left ...
Beverly and I knelt down and he put his big hands on our
heads and prayed a prayer of blessing over us ... I will
never forget that. I treasure that day more than words
can express. We were beginning our walk of faith!"*

- Jimmy Carroll

Story

Jimmy Carroll grew up in Raleigh, North Carolina. He was raised in
a Christian home and attended church every Sunday. He married his
childhood sweetheart that he met in the eighth grade. He accepted
Christ at the age of fifteen at a Word of Life camp, went to Liberty
University, accepted an internship to work at Thomas Road Baptist
Church, eventually moved to his home church, and became the co-
pastor. He was enjoying a twelve-year ministry at his home church and
did not really want for anything else in his ministry.

He had the girl, he had the ministry, he had the position—but he
didn't have the peace of God.

For several years, he felt unsettled.

Jimmy shares his heart:

For a few years, I felt God calling me to step out by
faith and plant a church. I would discount it as Satan

trying to destroy my life. The thoughts of the unknown and having to start over and struggle made it easy to stay in my place of comfort.

Although he know that God was calling him to take a step of faith and start a new work, Jimmy still had some conditions that God would have to accept. He tells of a conversation with a fellow kingdom builder:

One day, I was talking to my friend, a missionary in Mexico, and he asked me what I was going to do. I told him that I felt God calling me to plant a church, and I was willing if God would … you can fill in the blank … basically, if I had money, people, "security" … then I would do God a favor and start a church. For the first time, I heard myself say this, and I was sick and convicted. I had spent my life preaching about faith and obedience but was living by sight and in disobedience. I wish that I could say that I immediately surrendered, but …

A few months later, during Thanksgiving in 2004, Jimmy, his wife, Beverly, and their son, Austin, visited friends in Orlando. They visited Discovery Church, and it was there that Jimmy surrendered to God completely. He shares:

Before the service even began, I sat down and wept and told God, "The page is blank. You fill it in. I say 'yes' to whatever You want—no matter the cost or no matter the sacrifice. I am yours completely."

He continues,

One week later, I resigned my comfortable and secure church. The following Tuesday, we announced it to the church staff. The following Sunday we announced it to the church. And two weeks later, I preached my last message to a flock of people I had known for years and thought I would spend the rest of my life shepherding.

Leaving the security of a well-established ministry was one thing; knowing where God was going to place him was something totally different. Jimmy shares from his heart, "God was calling me 'to something,' not 'from something.' It was January 3, 2005—my first day since graduating from LU that I did not have a church or a group of people to shepherd ... I was faith-walking."

Several weeks later, Jimmy began the walk that God had laid out for him. Journey Church began in the party room of the Buffalo Lanes Bowling Center on Oak Forest Road in North Raleigh.

They met for the first time on February 27, 2005, with about ten families. That wasn't the official launch date, but it was simply the beginning of a six-month planning process to figure out what it was that they were setting out to do. They spent months developing a leadership team and planning for a September launch date. Along the way they met in several different places, including a hotel meeting room, another church building, and area homes. It was a time when God began to unite a group of people to make a difference in the North Raleigh area.

On September 18, 2005, Journey Church opened the doors for its first service at Millbrook Elementary School. Over 250 people showed up on that first Sunday.

From the very first day, Journey sensed the hand of God on the church and has been committed to following God's plan for the future. Each day brings a new excitement as people are connecting with God and others and pursuing a life of significance.

People and relationships are key to the development of Journey Church. Jimmy writes about those who came alongside to partner with this church plant:

> There are so many stories of people who were instrumental in the planting of Journey Church. This is one of the amazing things about this process.
>
> Paul Crouthamel, an alumnus of Liberty, moved his family from Maryland to be a part of Journey Church.

151

Paul and I only had a casual relationship, and I had met his wife only once. She had never been to Raleigh. I did not even know how many kids he had. By accident, I called him the day that I was going to resign and told him to drop everything and move down to help me plant a church in Raleigh. I was joking, of course, and laughing while I said it. However, he was dead quiet and asked if I was serious. I didn't know what to say. I said, 'No, not really ... but if you are considering it, then "yes" I am serious.' Two months later, he called to say he was coming to help us start Journey Church. Paul and his family moved to Raleigh in June of 2005. Paul now serves as our small groups pastor and is the campus pastor for our second campus.

Jimmy tells the story of another LU alumnus:

Rob Wetzel moved from Missouri to be a part of Journey Church. I had known and worked with Rob through the years, and he had a heart for God and for working with young people. Rob was without a job at the time and committed to come to Raleigh for the summer of 2005 to help in any way he could. We needed him, and he provided some great experience. After the summer, he and his family decided to move to Raleigh and become a permanent part of Journey Church. Now he serves on our staff as an associate pastor.

Jimmy goes on,

Paul Callaghan worked for me as a youth intern in 1994 and then served in several other churches in various roles. He also is a Liberty grad. Paul's wife, Blair, was actually in one of my youth groups. Paul and Blair were living in Orlando at the time. In reality, Paul is actually the only person that I begged to be a part of Journey Church. He is very creative, has an entrepreneurial spirit, and could sing and play the guitar. And we needed a worship leader. He moved to Raleigh in February of

2005 and now serves as our worship pastor—and is a volunteer by choice.

Mark Harvey is a former engineer and most recently a middle school math teacher. I had known Mark for many years, and when we started, he and his wife were one of our core families. Mark approached me and said that he felt led to go into full-time ministry, and he wanted to serve at Journey Church. He is now our business administrator.

Lisa Bauer is from Rustburg, Virginia, which is just outside of Lynchburg, and attended Thomas Road Baptist Church. Lisa actually had served with me at my home church. She felt led to be a part of Journey Church and has been with us from the beginning. Her husband, Dave, is in charge of our sound, lights, and video. Lisa now serves at my administrative assistant, and she is our Next Steps director.

Jimmy describes these as the main people who started with Journey Church and have since ended as staff members. In reviewing each of these, an interesting evidence of commitment occurred in that no one, including Jimmy, took a salary for the entire first year. Everybody walked their own journey of faith to have God meet their needs.

Key people were not the only highlight in the story of Journey Church. Jimmy states that beyond God, no one was more instrumental than his wife and son.

He shares from his heart

This was a family decision, and although it seems ridiculous now, we were prepared for it to just be the three of us for a while. We talked about doing Bible studies in our home until God brought us some people. But, as God can only do, of course, he brought more people.

My wife and son sacrificed a lot to make Journey a reality. We did door to door canvassing, together. We prayed together. And, we gave of our limited resources. I remember my son gave the first $20 ever given to Journey Church. What a gift and declaration that was for Beverly and me. This was a tough transition for him. At the age of thirteen, he willingly left everything and every friend he had ever known and moved to a new school, new home, new friends, and a new church—well, sort of a new church. He moved from a youth group of 150 students to a bowling alley with ten families. That had to be fun!

All I know is, I could not have done and still could not do what I do without them.

Those early days and those early decisions were tough. At times, Jimmy knew that God was leading, but he couldn't see what the next step was. Support was crucial, and it was there. However, Jimmy and Beverly wanted to make sure they were stepping out on faith and allow God to do what only God could do.

Jimmy recalls the struggle of trusting God and resting in His provision:

The church I left committed to support us with $3,000 per month for one year and to pay our insurance. Beverly and I never cashed one check. After several months, we returned the checks and got our own insurance. We were appreciative of their support and belief in us, but we felt that this journey required us to act by faith and put our full assurance in God.

After that decision, we had no idea how God would supply our needs. But we were confident in Him.

We cashed out our retirement accounts and planned to live off what little savings we had. During that time, I met with a dear friend who had planted a church over thirty years ago. His son, Chris, was also a church planter. David Rhodenhizer suggested that we apply to the Liberty Baptist Fellowship for support. LBF was established by Dr. Falwell in 1981 for the purpose of helping and funding local church plants in reaching their communities for Christ.

We applied and met with Dr. Falwell and the board in the spring of 2005. We told them of the dream we had and what we believed God wanted to do through us. They committed to support us for $1,000 per month for one year. It was a start, and we were so thankful for their support.

But worth far more than the support they gave us was what Dr. Falwell did before we left. He asked that Beverly and I kneel down. He put his big hands on our heads and prayed a prayer of blessing over us.

I will never forget that day as long as I live. I treasure that day more than words can express.

Strategy

The vision of Journey Church from the beginning has been to have a city-wide impact that would enable them to have a global impact. This can best be accomplished through the process of multiplication and duplication. Church planting is a strategic focus of Journey Church. Their vision is to plant churches all over the triangle area and together reach this region for Christ.

Jimmy is quick to articulate the reason for the existence of Journey Church. He states, "We say that our vision is to 'reach out—grow up.' In short, our mission is to 'help people follow Jesus.' While I think that we have done a pretty good job with some of this, one of our concerns is that we not just build a crowd but that we actually connect people with Jesus."

It began with ten families in a bowling alley on February 27, 2005. Jimmy Carroll chose Raleigh because it was his home city. Similar to the calling of Dr. Falwell, God gave Jimmy a very specific calling to capture his city for Christ.

It was launched in the northwest part of Raleigh at Millbrook Elementary School on September 18, 2005.

As with many church planters, Jimmy knew he wanted to impact a city for Christ, but he wasn't quite sure how to go about it. He shares some of his first thoughts:

> When I first started, I did not know much about church planting. What I did know is that the most effective strategy for impacting an entire city was to be one church in many locations. At the time, I did not even know that anybody else was developing a multisite strategy. I looked at the largest churches in our city, and while they had made a tremendous impact, in most cases, it was not citywide. Their impact was confined to their area of the city.

Jimmy knew that the mission was clear. As he has often told Journey Church, its purpose is to "help people follow Jesus." However, the question remained unanswered as to what was the most strategic way to accomplish this mission.

Jimmy again shares about the desire to see a city reached for Christ:

> In my research, I found out that what we wanted to do was not a new idea. I began learning about being a multisite church. We had not even launched our first campus and I knew that God was calling us to impact the entire city of Raleigh. We were not sure what the trigger would be to launch the second campus, but we had guessed that we would need to be running about 1,000 people and be at least five years old before launching the second campus. Our sense was that the next few campuses would happen much quicker. The larger we grew, the more opportunities we would have to expand.

Again, Jimmy was living by the conditions of Journey's growth and not the conviction of his faith. He was waiting for just the right pieces to fall into place before another campus would be started. For two years, this was the process—and this was the struggle: when would God be ready to open another site for Journey Church?

In May 2007, God used another opportunity to create a milestone in the ministry development of Journey Church and Jimmy Carroll. Jimmy recalls a trip back to Lynchburg to honor the one who had prayed over and blessed him and Beverly just two years prior. He shares:

> Dr. Falwell passed on May 15, 2007, and I went to Lynchburg to pay respects. I knew that I would not get to see the family. That's why you normally go to a funeral … to minister to the family. Yet I felt like God wanted me to go.
>
> This day was another turning point for me. While I stood there looking at Dr. Falwell lying in the casket, I reflecting about his influence in my life. I had been a student at Liberty University. I had served at TRBC as a youth intern. Beverly and I had received support from Liberty Baptist Fellowship, and I remembered his prayer of blessing over me.
>
> Then I was starting to think about his influence for the Kingdom of God … his character and integrity … the millions around the world who know Jesus because of his life.
>
> Then the reflection turned to conviction.
>
> The Holy Spirit started revealing to me how that what had started out as a journey of faith, trusting Him for everything, had already shifted to a place of comfort. I heard Him say to me in a clear voice, "Your dreams are too small." I started weeping, and I repented right there.

> I promised God that I would never again attempt anything that I could do without Him.
>
> I came back and, the next week, repented to my congregation, and I cast the vision that God birthed in me. We were going to plant church sites all over Raleigh and reach this city for Christ.

At the time Journey Church was averaging only 348 people. It was a far cry from the 1,000 people Jimmy had planned on before starting a second location. Jimmy remembers challenging his church to what God had called them to do. It was a step of faith. But more important, it was a step of obedience.

> Jimmy recalls, "I told them that we were going to launch our second campus in September 2008 and that we would be running 800 by the end of 2008. We launched our second campus on September 14, 2008, and we are averaging over 800 in November of 2008."

God was doing a work—and it required faith walking to do it.

Jimmy accepted a position on the board of Liberty Baptist Fellowship for the purpose of helping others plant churches and reach other cities for Christ.

> Again, he shares about this growing strategy:
>
> In addition to launching future Journey campuses in and around the Raleigh area, I feel God leading me to be involved in planting other churches, coaching and developing future church planters. I recently joined the board of the LBF (currently supporting twenty-seven church planters), and I am in discussions with a few other pastors about partnering together to plant autonomous churches nationally and internationally.

Currently, Journey Church meets at two locations, meeting four different times. Services are held at the northeast campus, called the "warehouse," on Saturday at 5:45 p.m., and Sunday at 9:15 a.m. and

11 a.m. The northwest campus meets in the Raleigh Grande Cinema 16 with services at 10 a.m. on Sundays.

Journey Northeast is the base of the church. The staging and lighting, as well as facilities, have a "permanent sense." The Saturday evening message is usually recorded and replayed at the other services and campus.

Journey Northwest meets in a sixteen-screen movie theater. Each Sunday, a dedicated crew arrives hours before the 10 a.m. start time to convert an entire side of the cineplex into a worship center, youth meeting rooms, child care, and nursery. The environment is warm and inviting, and the seating is comfortable.

The NW campus has a specific campus pastor, Paul Crouthamel, their own worship team, as well as hosts, greeters, and additional workers.

Set-up begins early with the renovation of the theater lobby into a welcome center featuring a small resource table, books, coffee bar and information table. With the Raleigh Grande Cinema functioning as a working movie theater, tear down is just as critical ... movie times begin as early as noon on Sunday afternoons.

Thorften Keffler, manager of the Raleigh Grande, feels that Journey Northwest has their organization and strategy down to a science. He states, "The setup and teardown is a credit to their (Journey Church's) attention to detail and organization." When asked about their impact on the community, he says, "Compared to other churches that have been here, they are some of the friendliest people I've ever met. They are very attentive to those who are visiting." He continues, "They are very caring of me and help out as much as they can."

Rochelle Fletcher is a hostess and greeter at Journey NW. She and her husband, Billy, have been attending for over a year with their four children. Rochelle shares that on the first Sunday, her youngest child said, "Mommy, that's church." As an African American, she also feels that race is a "non-issue" in this church.

She recalls the first time she met Pastor Jimmy's dad, who is a greeter for Journey NW. "I knew from the moment he shook my hand that there was a genuine love in this place; it is a place of real acceptance."

Although there are two campuses with multiple services, there is also a focused attention on forming community within the church. A recent praise and worship night featured all campuses and services joining together as one. Pastor Jimmy commented on the night in a recent blog posted at www.jimmycarroll.org: "We closed out the weekend with a night of worship. It was out of control. It is so weird that we can have that much fun while praising our King. The room was packed, and the energy was contagious. I think Jesus was pleased."

In addition to joint events, there is a strategy to make sure all those who volunteer and minister at both campuses share a common purpose and vision.

Kirt Storch is a host leader at Journey Northwest. When asked about the purpose of Journey Church, he replied, "We reach people and grow them up in Christ."

Greg Margosian and his wife, Tracey, also serve at Journey Northwest. Greg feels that the church "works hard at building community." He feels there is a good balance between discipleship and winning people. He also senses that Journey Church, with its leadership, is "very intentional in encouraging people in their walk … wherever they are in their walk."

Successes

Two words summarize the successes of Journey Church: faith and focus.

Journey Church has continued to grow and be successful because they have refused to settle and become complacent with the typical growth that occurs in the walls of a church.

Jimmy shares about this commitment to faith walking, "We have from the beginning and continue to take risks and operate in a realm of faith. Our entire short history has been something that only God could do."

Another reason for Journey's success has been their high level of focus. Jimmy talks about the early years,

> We chose early on to operate under a "less is more" philosophy. We do a few things and do them well. We are obsessed with the vision of "reach out and grow up." This is the mission of helping people follow Jesus. Everything gets filtered through that, and if it will not help us accomplish this mission, we don't do it.

For many church plants, this commitment to a missions approach to ministry is something that is lacking. There develops a perceived need to do all that you can ... in order to reach everyone that you can. A ministry struggles to be defined by a simple mission and focused vision.

Jimmy communicates this struggle:

> We have sacrificed the good for the best. The enemy of the best is often the good. We have watched a lot of church plants try to immediately be everything to everybody. This caused them to fail in being focused on their purpose. In order to stop this, we said no.

> I think you are defined by your "no." You can't say no until you figure out when to say yes. We said yes early on to a few things and have said no many times since then."

Jimmy gives a few examples of staying focused and operating in the realm of faith. In the area of staff, Journey staffs for where they are going instead of where they are. This demands a clear mission statement as to what the church sees as their primary calling and the necessary commitment to accomplish that calling.

Whether it is starting a service before it is really needed or leasing a space after one year of existence, Journey Church believes its success has been in staying focused and walking by faith.

Jimmy describes this balance of risk and faith: "Our entire journey has been God calling us to the next level and us trusting Him to get us there."

Struggles

Journey Church faces many of the same struggles that many church plants face in the area of leadership development and volunteer support. Jimmy shares some thoughts:

> Because our church is so young and we have so many young Christians and non-Christians, we struggle with the proverbial 80-20 rule. We have about 20 percent of the people who are doing about 80 percent of the work. Those 20 percent are also giving about 80 percent of the money. We have not had time to let the maturity catch up with the numerical growth.

As with many young churches, the enthusiasm is high, and the entrepreneurial spirit, infectious. The excitement of creating ways to reach people and the anticipation of having them come to Christ often takes precedence over their development and growth as disciples.

The "sizzle" becomes more appealing than the "steak"—but the "steak" is where the nourishment comes from and growth takes place.

Jimmy validates this concern: "Our vision is 'Reach out—Grow up.' We have been much more successful at the reaching than the growing. It is a constant struggle to recruit and develop volunteers to serve. Just when we start to catch up, our attendance jumps, and we are again unhealthy."

He continues,

> The other aspect of this is the spiritual growth … Our mission is to "help people follow Jesus," so we are

constantly looking for better ways to accomplish this. We started out saying we were only going to do small groups to accomplish this but are now looking to expand our process to help grow people. We can do this by adding mentoring groups and in-depth studies. These are two things that we are looking to add to our process.

Significance

Journey Church is significant in its commitment to a multisite strategy, its adherence to its mission and vision, and the priority it places on its people to grow up and serve in Christ.

Journey has identified the service that those in the body of Christ share as being an overflow of their relationship with Christ. At Journey, they love to witness "overflow." They define overflow as being the point where God does a work in one's heart and life so that it spills over into the lives of the people around them.

Every person is encouraged to take part in volunteering in some form of ministry through a ministry team. By joining a ministry team at Journey, they will experience, through hands-on ministry, the transformation of both their own life and the lives of others that they serve.

This shared or overflow ministry provides each person with the continual growth in the body.

> "Serving on the First Impressions ministry team is my chance to love people, to make new friends, and show the love of Christ to each person right where they are."
>
> *Carolyn*

> "I have never been part of a worship team that has such a heart for God and a heart for worship. What we experience together each week is truly amazing. There is nothing I'd rather be doing."
>
> *Karen*

"Volunteering has helped me connect with others and has helped me connect with God in a way I never knew would be possible in working with kids."

Justin

Each person reflects the vision and mission of Journey Church through their commitment to Christ and their service for others.

Summary

As a church planter, Jimmy stresses being assured of one's calling and giftedness. He states,

> The best advice I can give a church planter is to begin by figuring out what you care about. What you care about is what you would do for free. It's what drives you. It's what you wake up thinking about. It's what you are obsessed over. What you care about is just as important as what you believe.

He continues with an analogy that summarizes the reality of faith and works:

> Most planters don't struggle with what they believe. Who cares if you believe that someone is hungry, but you don't care enough to feed them? Who cares if you believe that someone needs to accept Christ in order to go to heaven, but you don't care enough to tell them? When you work for someone else, you don't get to decide what you care about. You have to care about what they care about, or you will not be successful in that organization. You can't have different agendas.

Jimmy continues about sharing the passion of the One who has called you:

> You have to be passionate about what they are passionate about. Most church planters who fail, do so because they have not figured out what they really care about.

They are not leading from a place of authenticity: authenticity about your passion, authenticity about your desires, and authenticity about your calling. When you figure this out, you don't have to manufacture passion. It is part of the overflow of your life. You are real, and people will see that and be inspired to follow. You are not trying to be someone else or just do a cool church plant. You are obsessed and passionate about Jesus and what He is doing in your life and what He has burned in your heart.

Jimmy has also find that a strong "yes" is found in a stronger "no." Too often, church planters try to do it all and be a church for all people. He offers some words about being focused in your philosophy:

"I would also encourage a church planter to operate with a 'less is more' philosophy. Once you figure out what is important, do that and nothing else. Don't try to be a full-service church. Do a few things, and do them well."

This commitment to singular focus and excellence is seen throughout the ministry of Journey Church. Whether it's a message series, a website, printed material, small group structure, setting up or tearing down, every aspect of their ministry is marked by an attention to detail and a commitment to excellence.

Soul

The soul of Journey Church is the commitment and abandonment to a vision that drives every other aspect of the ministry. This vision, coupled with a mission that is simple and clear, provides Journey Church with a passion to reach the community of Raleigh for Christ.

Jimmy talks about this vision:

Our vision is Reach Out—Grow Up. The mission is to "help people follow Jesus." We define a "follower" as one who is getting to know Him and who is responsive. This is more than a slogan for us.

I am obsessed with helping people follow Jesus. Everything we do is filtered through that lens ... every song ... every message ... the volume ... the light settings ... programming ... our meetings ... everything is intentional. We say no more than we say yes. We are focused and passionate about reaching lost people and helping them grow as followers. This is what we bleed. You will constantly hear us say, "Just say yes to Jesus. As He reveals Himself, take the next step, whatever the next step is. That's our purpose. That's our passion!"

Statistics and Structure

Journey Church, counting all campuses, currently averages $18,000 per week in offering. Ten percent of all offerings is designated to church planting and missions. They currently spend about $18,000 per month on rent between the two locations.

Apart from initial funding from Liberty Baptist Fellowship, Journey Church has never received consistent outside support from any source other than tithes and offerings. All staff went one year without salary. This enabled Journey Church to put more money into equipment, marketing, and other start-up costs. Journey Church currently has seven full-time staff, four part-time staff, and over 300 volunteers.

In September 2005, attendance began with 166. In 2006, attendance averaged 265; 2007 averaged 400 (a second location was added in September 2007); attendance in 2008 averaged 650.

Journey is a pastor/staff led church where members of the pastoral staff are considered elders.

Their style of worship is a rock band similar to Hillsong and Passion. It is described as very worshipful. There is only corporate worship with no special music or performance-style music. Teaching is focused on life change, extremely practical and biblical. There is use of creative styles of teaching with props and video. The target audience is "to help people follow Jesus", therefore there is weekly sensitivity to non-Christians and unchurched.

ABOUT THE CHURCH PLANTER—

Jimmy Carroll is founding and Lead Pastor of Journey Church (www. takeajourney.org), an independent, non-denominational church in Raleigh, North Carolina. The vision of Journey Church is "Reach Out—Grow Up."

Their mission is to help people follow Jesus. A follower of Jesus is defined as someone who gets to know Him and responds.

Jimmy and his wife Beverly grew up in Raleigh and have served together in ministry since 1989.

Pastor Carroll is a 1990 graduate of Liberty University in Lynchburg, Virginia (B.S., Church Ministries). He was ordained in Basset, Virginia, in 1993.

He regularly writes a blog, www.jimmycarroll.org. Jimmy also serves on the Board of Liberty Baptist Fellowship, a church planting ministry of Thomas Road Baptist Church and Liberty University.

Jimmy and Beverly were childhood sweethearts, and both began their relationship with God as teenagers. They were married in 1989 and have one son, Austin (1991).

Chapter 12
Finding Your Place in the Center

"Batman had Robin. The Lone Ranger had Tonto. Tarzan had Jane. Even those who start out in life trying to make it on their own find out they need someone next to them to share life's moments. God is a God of relationships and He's created you to be connected to others who are seeking Him."

- Center Point Church in Lexington

Story

Tim Parsons, after being in full-time youth ministry for more than twenty years, decided God was calling him to plant a church. He read everything he could get his hands on, talked to people who had planted churches, and attended every seminar he could find—yet he chose to start Center Point Church in a very unconventional way. He calls it "Kamikaze Church Planting": you just start. Do or die ... you just start.

Tim Parsons grew up in a ministry home. His dad was a pastor for forty years, serving in local churches. Tim grew up seeing ministry up close and personal. Often it was good, and sometimes it was bad and even ugly.

Tim received Christ as Savior at age seven and began a lifetime of seeking God. After graduating high school, he enrolled in Liberty Baptist College (now Liberty University) and was presented with the concept of a youth ministry for the first time. It was there that God confirmed his call to ministry. While at Liberty, Tim had opportunities to develop ministry skills while serving as an intern in the college department at Thomas Road Baptist Church and traveling on an evangelistic ministry team. God continued to use these opportunities to confirm his lifelong call to ministry. While at Liberty, time also met his wife, Susan (Fry).

Following his graduation and ordination in 1985, Tim served in several youth ministry positions in Kentucky and Florida. While in Florida, he oversaw a local church youth ministry consisting of nearly 1,000 students at Idlewild Baptist Church of Tampa. In the course of his career, Tim became a recognized speaker at camps and retreats. In addition he has trained youth leaders in seven countries and taught as a professor in a Christian college.

After completing twenty years in youth ministry, Tim sensed God's call on him and a team of three other men to plant Center Point Church of Lexington in 2005, where he currently serves as lead pastor.

Planting a church was the last thing on Tim's mind. He shares,

> I thought I would always work with students, and I planned my life that way. But God had something different in store for me. It all began in 1997 when several of my friends were called to plant West Ridge Church (westridge.com; see chapter 8). While working as a professor at Lexington Baptist College, I took a trip with colleagues and students to help West Ridge launch their first service. God used the experiences of that trip—going door to door, helping the setup crew, and witnessing the first service—to begin His work in my life.

In 2003, Tim began to sense that God was stirring his heart. Through a series of experiences, new ministry opportunities, and a focused prayer effort, God began to bring clear direction to Tim. He relates,

> Strangely enough, friends had begun suggesting that I consider pastoring a church, and this idea was so strange to me. While I was spending time with my thirteen-year-old daughter Kasey, she said, "Dad, I don't

want to move and leave my friends, but I know God is calling us to move and start a church." Soon after, my wife confirmed her sentiments. Everyone seemed to know ... everyone but me! The situation really upset me, so in time with the Lord, I prayed and said, "God, I will quit my job and move and plant a church if that is your will for me. But that is so radical—I have to know it is from you! My heart is so unsettled, and I am upset nearly every day. Here is how I will know it is from you—if you will give me total peace in my heart about this decision for a period of seven days, I will confidently follow you and plant a church."

For the next couple of days I forgot all about it—then I began to notice the peace in my heart, which continued for the rest of the week. It was the first time I had been at peace since the conception of the idea in my heart. God confirmed His calling in my life. Since then, I have doubted my ability on almost a daily basis. While I have doubted my worthiness and how God would provide, I have never questioned, for even one second, God's call or what He wanted me to do! This has provided me with incredible peace.

Tim had the assurance he needed from God to step out and obey the calling. He then wanted to know that his pastor and new team were with him. Tim shares,

Now that I knew what God was calling me to do, the hardest parts of pursuing it lie ahead. Even though the plant was a year away, I knew the right thing to do was to talk with the pastor. I also knew that this could mean immediate termination. I made an appointment with him in June of 2004 and told him what God was doing in my life—how God had called me to plant a church in June of 2005. He confirmed this calling in my life and made provision for a yearlong transition. Since, he has become one of our most faithful supporters. In January of 2005, I began the process of training and planning for several days a week. The team was assembled, and we met numerous times to chart our course. Weekly, we spent an hour in prayer by telephone. After confirming the city to which God was calling us, we all moved to Lexington, Kentucky, in June 2005 and launched Center Point Church in September.

Strategy

Planting Center Point Church became an incredible learning experience for Tim and his team. When God called him to be a part of planting a church, Tim read everything he could get his hands on about church planting. He attended conferences, interviewed planters, and asked questions of anyone who would answer him. God began to formulate His plan for this church in Tim's mind.

Tim chose the city of Lexington after much prayer and consideration. God laid Lexington on his heart early in 2004. He came to the area for a job interview and was moved while driving around the city. He found himself weeping for no known reason and burdened for the city. Tim and his team were asked to consider other cities and areas, but God had left a profound impression on him. Lexington was the place where he would plant a church.

Center Point started in a very unconventional way. Most churches start after a core is formed and developed. There are informational meetings and in-home meetings. There are pre-launch dinners and an official launch Sunday. Tim started Center Point is different way. He shares from his heart:

> I often say that we started Center Point "kamikaze style." Center Point began with a team of four. Each of us moved to Lexington in the summer of 2005. We hit it with a vengeance! To help get us started, we had five different church groups come to Lexington. They stayed with us in our homes, we fed them, and we all worked together. We sponsored four "Vacation Bible School" style projects in local parks that we called

Upside Down. We also sponsored a local sports camp. We put up signs, passed out fliers and met people in the community. We all wore bright Center Point T-shirts to get people's attention. We also began serving the community with various projects like carrying out people's groceries, meeting needs, and placing door hanger advertisements on homes. We took what little money we had and blitzed the area with advertisement with four mailers, many road signs, and radio advertisement. We told everyone we were starting in the Regal Cinemas on September 11, 2005. We prayed for 200 and had 201. God was faithful, and we were on our way.

To date, their strategy has not significantly changed. They are still pursuing the original plans and methods with which God challenged them.

Center Point provides two services on Sunday morning at 9:15 and 11. Dress and atmosphere are casual and welcoming. Every two months, the church provides an opportunity to learn about the vision, mission, and values of Center Point. It gives people the chance to "check it out" and see if Center Point is for them.

Tim has also established Connect Groups which meet during the week. Connecting with others gives CP members three important benefits: encouragement through life's challenges, accountability to take people to the next level, and friendship they can count on no matter what. These Connect Groups become a place to belong at Center Point, a place where everybody's name is known.

Although Center Point has not yet planted a daughter church, they have been saving for the project since their first Sunday. When God opens the door, they are ready to walk through. In the mean time, they have partnered with ICM (International Cooperating Ministries) and have raised the money to build four churches—in Bangladesh, India, Nepal, and Rwanda.

Successes

To this point, the successes of Center Point Church can be measured not in buildings or budgets but in the lives of the people God has changed. To share those changes, Center Point has created a marketing plan and started a website, www.whosavedmylife.com. Traffic is driven to this site through billboards, cards, T-shirts and other promotional material. The site shares some of the remarkable stories of God's work and grace through the ministry of Center Point.

One such story is that of Joey and Sara. Joey and Sara came to Center Point on its third Sunday as guests of some friends. At first look, they were an outgoing couple who were just married and eager to take on life and its challenges. They were attractive, and everything seemed to be going their way. The real story, however, was quite different. Joey shares his experience from www.whosavemylife.com:

> I was about to lose it all … my wife, family, in-laws, home, job, and even my mind when I called out for help from a bed at an alcohol and drug treatment center to a God that I didn't know or understand. This was on September 20, 2005. It was the twelfth day that I had spent in the facility, and I had not yet been able to catch a wink of sleep. Not to mention that I had lost control of my central nervous system. As a result, I could hardly walk and was constantly drenched with sweat. Believing that I was having a heart attack a few days prior, I had been rushed to the hospital. A fellow patient at the alcohol and drug treatment center told me that I was de-toxing from benzodiazepines. It was the closest thing to hell I had ever experienced. But on this night more than any other, the fear, anxiety, and hopelessness of the direction of my life crippled. It was so much that I didn't care if I even saw the morning. I had given up, thrown in the towel, and as I lay in a bed staring at a ceiling unable to sleep, I called out one last time for help.

I was twenty-nine years old, and although my home life as a child was filled with love and support, somewhere along the way I lost my own significance and self-esteem. I longed for acceptance by others and was willing to place blame for my failures on anyone other than myself. I was caught in traps. I believed so many lies about myself that the only coping mechanism I had left was alcohol and drugs. Since I was fifteen, the longest that I had stayed sober was two and a half years, and that relapse landed me in my third treatment program.

After leaving the treatment center on October 7, 2005, I returned to my home in Lexington, Kentucky. There I was given ultimatums by my wife, family, and employer that I had zero chances remaining, which ultimately meant that I would be divorced and homeless. I had to stay sober. I knew that God had helped me that night I cried out to Him at the treatment center, and I knew that on my own will, I would not survive another week.

About this time, we were asked by some friends to try out a new church, Center Point Church of Lexington that had started at the Regal Cinemas in Hamburg Place. My wife and I decided we had nothing to lose. We were only four months into our marriage and I had spent 28 of those days in treatment.

The leadership team of Center Point reached out to my family and has to this day never let go of us. They also hold me accountable for the commitments I make. Members of the church have supported my recovery and have never once judged the bad choices and decisions I've made. Although many of them have never walked in my shoes, they do their best to relate areas in their lives with which they struggle and the victory they've received through Christ.

My wife and I accepted Christ in November 2005, and that decision has led us down a road to healing and freedom from bondage. We host a Connect Group which is a small group of church members that get together to discuss the message from the past Sunday and how we can apply it to our daily walk. The weekly sermons speak to my personal situation, and the small groups help me with the challenges of my life. Our leadership team and church family are concerned for people who do not know Jesus Christ. In our church it is possible to talk with others about personal issues, and the church leaders serve as strong spiritual examples to all of us.

One of the people that Joey has been used by God to help save is Victor. Tim met Victor while working at a local cemetery—one of those jobs a church planter needs to take once in a while. Almost immediately Victor began asking questions about God. Tim relates Victor's story:

We talked openly until we were told we could no longer talk at work. Instead, we began meeting for lunch to talk. After losing touch with Victor for a few months, I called him and invited him to help with a Christmas project. Victor came, meeting many of the folks at Center Point. He promised to come to our Christmas service that year. But, like many times before, he didn't show up. A day or so later, I called to invite him and his wife to a Christmas Eve outreach it was then that his wife, Amy, told me that Victor was dying. He had been rushed to the hospital with a ruptured bowel. I immediately went to the hospital to see him. I continued to visit him and Amy there nearly every day for the next few months. It was on the day that Victor was being discharged that he invited Christ into his life as Savior. I set up a time to come by his house and begin discipleship the next week. But he was too sick to really talk. I left the materials and planned to come back in a few days. On my next visit, Victor asked me to share Christ with Amy. I told Amy how Jesus loved her and wanted to change her life. Strangely, I noticed that she quoted the verses with me as I shared them. This struck me oddly since I knew she was unchurched. When I asked her if she wanted to invite Christ into her life, she said that she already had. She had picked up the book I left and had gone through the first chapter on salvation. The reason she knew the verses is because she had read them over and over.

Since then I have had the privilege of discipling a healthy Victor and an inquiring Amy and have seen them grow in unbelievable ways. Joey has also been a part of this process. There have been many like Joey and Sara and Victor and Amy. The successes of Center Point lie in the lives that God has changed here.

Struggles

As with any church plant, mistakes have been made, and struggles follow. Tim feels that one such issue occurred early in the development of Center Point. In many church plants, there is funding available for the lead pastor to concentrate exclusively on the growth and needs of the church plant. Tim instead made the decision to work full-time and have other staff receive compensation. Tim shares his heart: "I learned what a mistake it was to work in the early months of planting CPC. I was not available to meet with people and pastor the way I needed to—it set us back a year or so."

Another area that Tim admitted was a struggle was in exercising prayer in the selection of leaders within the church. Again, from his heart, Tim shares,

Although God sent us a great team, I did not pray like I should have before selecting it. Jesus went to the mountains and prayed all night before selecting His team—I did not give it the priority it required. Since

177

then, we pray extensively before adding anyone to the makeup of leadership at Center Point.

An ongoing struggle is with the city and culture of Lexington itself. Tim shares that Lexington is a difficult city in which to plant a church. It is loaded with churches, and most people attend one of them out of duty or habit. The area of changed lives and response to truth is a burden to Tim and the leadership of Center Point. Tim shares,

> Our city is deprived of truth. Sadly, most truth-driven churches are dried up. There is a lot of error here, and it is hard to fight. Often I feel like we are fighting hell by the acre. Because of this, we hold to our vision, "We are a church where you can experience love and belonging while learning truth and finding hope."

Significance

Pastor Tim wraps up the importance and significance of teaching truth at Center Point. He illustrates in some brief statements:

> When God called us to plant, He formulated several ideas in our minds, and through several long meetings we have been able to put them on paper. Our goal was to create a church where you can experience love and belonging while learning truth and finding hope. For us, that goal translates daily into the mission to take everyone we meet *one step closer* to becoming a true disciple of Jesus Christ. This makes Center Point a church where "truth" is a nonnegotiable value and changing lives is the main thing. This seems different from many churches where program, buildings, and budgets seem to get the main stage. We have seen this model work! Although it may not grow as fast as other models, God is using it to radically impact people.

Summary

Tim relates two primary lessons that he has learned in planting a church after twenty-five years of ministry. He emphasizes the importance of staying focused on vision and mission. The distractions of planting and building a church are never-ending, time-consuming, and always urgent. Understand what your priority is, and stay on task.

Additionally, Tim encourages church planters to have only one job, if at all possible. "I made a big mistake early on by working a different job rather than having a dedicated focus on the church."

Tim also mentions the precedence of prayer in the selection of leadership. He writes, "I learned the priority of seeking God earnestly before adding anyone to leadership. If Jesus did it before choosing the disciples, I need to do it for the leadership of Center Point."

Soul

Tim shares the driving motivation of Center Point:

> The heartbeat of Center Point is life change—seeing people move on in their faith. We are passionate about truth, families, and reaching the unchurched of Lexington. Our goal is to move people through the process of HEARING THEN APPLYING THEN LIVING. This is evidenced by hearing the truth on Sundays at The Entry Point, our main service, applying in Connect Groups, and living it out through sharing and serving.

Statistics and Structure

Center Point had 201 on its Launch Sunday. Attendance then dropped 100. Most of those 100 were unchurched people. Year two saw attendance rise from 130 per week to 175 per week. Right before Center Point's third birthday, they moved into a "temporary-permanent" location. This location is a leased storefront.

Center Point Church is a nontraditional Southern Baptist Church. No support was garnered from the Association. Tim Parsons began Center Point with the help of several private donors as well as three churches: Idlewild Baptist Church in Tampa, Florida, West Ridge Church in metro Atlanta, and First Baptist Church of Brooksville, Florida. Center Point was planted by the families of four men: Todd Anders, Sergio Mendoza, Todd Thomas, and Tim Parsons.

Center Point is led by a pastoral team that makes decisions as a unit. This team is guided by a leadership team made up of men from the church. There are also several Collaboration Teams (creative, financial resource, facility, community, and missions) that guide the leading teams and provide insight to the church. Center Point functions with over seventy-five people serving regularly. These teams meet monthly for Servant Leadership Gathering, which is a time for a meal, fellowship, worship, discussion, and training.

Center Point's worship is varied, but designed to be engaging and comfortable to a lost person. The environment is friendly and contemporary. The teaching style is truth heavy but relaxed in presentation. Teaching is always exegetical, but is presented in four different formats: life issue studies, book studies, Bible character studies, and theological concept studies.

ABOUT THE CHURCH PLANTER—

Tim Parsons is the Lead Pastor of Center Point Church of Lexington (www.cplex.org), a non-traditional Southern Baptist Church in Lexington, Kentucky, where people can experience love and belonging while learning truth and finding hope. Their mission is to take everyone they meet one step closer to becoming a true disciple of Jesus Christ.

Tim is a well-recognized speaker and former college professor.

Pastor Parsons is a graduate of Liberty University in Lynchburg, Virginia (B.S., Youth Ministry) and Lexington Baptist College (M.A.,

Biblical Studies). He was ordained at Bethel View Baptist Church in Bristol, Tennessee, in 1985.

Married since 1985, Tim and Susan (Fry) have three children: Kasey (1991), Nick (1996), and Sara (1998).

Chapter 13
Following Footsteps

*"My father always told me,
'Find a job you love and you'll never have
to work a day in your life.'"*

- Jim Fox

Story

Chris Rhodenhizer grew up in a Christian home. In fact, he grew up in a home of a church planter. When Chris was five, his dad, Dr. David Rhodenhizer, moved their family to Alexandria, Virginia, and planted a church (see chapter 3).

Chris said, "I have had the privilege of watching my dad start and lead a church. This is one of the things which fueled my passion to start and lead a church."

Passion is a critical component in Chris's life. He has seen it modeled and demonstrated in many of the men he has followed. However, he knows that his passion for life and for ministry came from one source:

Although God has given me this passion, it truly wasn't my passion until I was seventeen. It was then that I realized the truth of the Gospel, my own sin, the cross of Jesus Christ, and my need to repent and submit to Jesus. It was then that God began His work in my life, and soon after gave me a call and a passion for ministry.

Chris enrolled in Liberty University to pursue a degree in religion with an emphasis in youth ministry. In those early years at Liberty God fueled his passion and created a vision in his heart. Chris followed the example of a leader who would have a profound influence on his life.

"I was able to see what a God-given call and vision could truly become when you are faithful to that call. The greatest example was Jerry Falwell. Dr. Falwell's vision was amazing!"

Chris began serving in churches as a youth pastor and young adult pastor. He enjoyed the ministry in the walls of the church and felt growth as he ministered. In 2005, Chris began working for his father as a young adult campus pastor at Calvary Road Baptist Church.

It was there that God began to do a renewing and stretching work in his heart:

> God began to move me to plant a church. We decided to launch the campus I was currently pastoring into its own church plant. My father was very helpful and led Calvary Road to support our launch prayerfully and financially. Image Church will forever be grateful for that starting point!

Strategy

In January of 2006, Chris and his wife met with a core leadership team of about fifteen in their home to cast a vision and make plans on how, when, and where in Northern Virginia to launch this new church.

Their first step was to gather interest. In February of 2006, they held an informational meeting in a gymnasium and had forty people in attendance. The meeting produced a good deal of interest, and Chris decided God was moving them to the next level. He shares his comments:

> After that meeting I began to search for a facility in which to gather our church. In March of 2006 we signed a lease with a school building and set a date to launch the first Sunday in April of 2006. Our team was

> so excited, and I was ready to go. Then came that phone call … you know, the one you dread ever getting.

It was the Friday before the launch of the church. The newly formed worship band was practicing in the basement of one of Chris's friends. Chris was reviewing his sermon, and there was great anticipation and excitement in the air as to what God was going to do with this new church.

Chris's cell phone rang, and when he answered the phone, the voice on the other end gave him news he had never anticipated hearing. He shares about that Friday night call:

> It was the lady our church had signed a lease with for our meeting space at the school. She began to share with me that we would not be able to meet there that coming Sunday. She also said that she needed to break the lease with us. Now, I cannot even begin to explain to you what my stomach did. My stomach was in knots. Every fear I had dreamed about was coming into my mind. How could God be in this? After questioning her, I hung up the phone. It then began to sink in … Image Church had people planning on showing up at a facility on Sunday … that no longer existed! I immediately hit my knees, and God took me to a place in my prayer life that I had never experienced before. He, told me that this was not about me, this would not be planted on Chris Rhodenhizer's strengths and abilities, and that this church would be much bigger than my leadership ability.

After spending a significant time in prayer, Chris proceeded to tell some of his leadership what had happened. It was a make or break time. Was Image Church about this young pastor who had a passion? Was it about the band and worship team? Was it about a great facility and creative approach to ministry? The answer to all of these questions was no … it was about God and what He wanted to do. It was His church. It was His passion to reach a lost community.

Chris and his team all got on the phone, and within twenty-four hours they had found a facility to use that was diagonally across the street from the original space … it had more space, it was already a church building, and it reduced the amount of setup to be done each week. God had answered their prayers. Chris sums it up, "God planted this church, not me!"

Image leased space, on Sunday evenings, from another church for eighteen months. Those were some of the toughest times that Chris had ever experienced. Three months into it, Chris and his elders knew they needed to find a space of their own to gather in. They felt that Sunday evenings were not a good meeting time for church.

Chris explains,

"In a situation like this, it was hard to move people to mission and create vision. Also, sometimes the church we were leasing from had their events taking place. To complicate the issue, we were not in the geographic area we truly desired to be in. But finding space for a church in the Northern Virginia/DC Metro area is not an easy task. Everything was expensive, and landlords typically did not want churches meeting in their spaces.

God was not only stretching Image Church in the need of a facility, He was doing it other ways also. Attendance was sporadic and inconsistent at best. On their first Sunday, they had 153 in attendance. Week two saw 132. For a number of weeks the attendance hovered just at 100. And then a string of weeks averaged at 130. This was a challenge to Chris, and God began to work in his heart again.

Chris relates his struggle,

What God did in me was reveal that I was to minister and serve right where I was. It didn't matter whether there were 100 people or 1,000 people. God had called me to proclaim the Gospel, to equip others to proclaim the Gospel and to move whatever size church, wherever we were meeting, to His mission. So I began to remove my focus from finding a space, to focus on equipping our church to be missional. About six months in we began to see more people coming to Jesus and getting baptized, we began to see some young men called into ministry, we sent out and supported a couple of missionaries, a couple ladies in our church got passionate about an orphanage we were supporting, and Image Church put together a 5K called I-Race—our little church raised several thousand dollars in missions—God was truly moving. Before I could even realize it, our church was living and acting like the church is supposed to live and act like! It had been just over a year, and God had done a work only He could accomplish.

Chris had found his stride in trusting God for the growth and purpose of Image Church. Then in the spring of 2007 he received another phone call.

Chris tells about this miracle call:

I was sitting in my office, which at the time was in my basement, and the phone rang. It was my father. He asked me to come by his office, which was about a 25 minute drive from my house. I was reluctant, but he said I really should come, and he thought it would benefit me to do so. I hopped in the car and drove to Alexandria.

When I arrived, my mom and dad were seated in his office talking with a sweet lady. I was introduced and thought she looked familiar. Although I couldn't place her, I remembered her face. I had run into her at a local grocery store some months before this meeting. She began to remind me of that day. I remembered I had my son, Liam, with me, and she had enjoyed meeting him, as well. She also told me she had heard me speak about Image Church, our vision, and our need for a meeting space. She then gave me something that I will never forget.

She handed me a gift of $116,000. I looked at the middle line, and it read, "One Hundred and Sixteen Thousand Dollars." She said that God had burdened her heart to help a church. When she ran into me at the grocery store, God wouldn't let her forget the young church called Image that needed a place to meet. So our church could now get a space in which to gather. I was floored and realized only God could have orchestrated this!

So after a long summer of searching, Image Church was able to relocate to a 23,000-square-foot warehouse in Dumfries, Virginia. God provided the warehouse and two additional staff.

Successes

The vision of Image Church has been clearly and simply presented. It is apparent in the selection of their name: A COMMUNITY OF PEOPLE REFLECTING THE IMAGE OF CHRIST.

The vision of the church is lived out through a simple process and values which become their mantra for life. Chris says, "We value ministry *Centered in Worship*, *Cultivated through Community*, and *Committed to Service*. The desire of Image is to see people lead lives of worship, live in community with other believers, and serve the church and the world by being and making disciples."

The ministry of Image Church is evidenced by the way lives are being changed and people are becoming more like Christ. Chris writes in a recent blog posting on what God is doing at Image Church:

Completely blown away, I don't even know where to start or how to express what happened yesterday! Our team had prayed hard all weekend for the Holy Spirit to move and work, and He definitely answered that prayer. I knew ahead of time that there were a lot of things going on in our church body. I had been praying about these things on Friday, and I realized that there was going to be something great coming on Sunday. So here is how God worked in His church yesterday:

- One person committed her life to Jesus Christ!

- A couple of people repented of some things.

- One person repented and sought prayer by a few of our elders.

- A couple of people were seeking to get things right in their relationship.

- Hurting people opened up and asked for prayer for things that are very deep.

- The crowd that gathered was lower than usual, but larger than three months ago and desired God to do an even bigger work in their lives.

- The music was passionate and worshipful, the prayer time moved us, the offering was generous, the WORD was proclaimed, the blood washed us, and we left changed!!!

Keep praying, keep worshiping, and keep reflecting HIS Image!

Image Church also places a strong emphasis on reaching out into the community with unique opportunities to show God's love. Chris published a blog posting about the Image Church sponsored I-Race:

WOW! I have been amazed all day at what took place this morning. I knew i-Race would be a great event, but I had no idea it would have the amount of runners we had and the amount of money that came in. We had between 40 and 50 people race, about 50 volunteers. As of right now we have brought in $4,300 for Manna (a food bank ministry), and I had no clue who half the people at the race were. This was truly a great event: our church came together, we reached into our community, and we fed kids around the world!

Chris continues to look for ways to teach many of the young believers the basics of their faith in Christ. As with many young church planters, creativity and unique teaching techniques are used to keep the interest level high. Chris, however, began to teach the basic doctrines of the faith and the statement of beliefs to his church without using the Sunday teaching time. Each week, Chris used his blog, "Imagine this ..." to highlight a specific doctrine or fundamental of the faith. It was not a long teaching but more of an explanation as to the truth, the importance of the Biblical truth to the believer, and a practical demonstration that could be applied to the life of the believer. These teaching blogs provided a creative and contemporary way to teach the unchanging truth.

The following is one of many short doctrinal lessons posted on Chris's blog. This one is foundational.

We believe the Holy Scriptures of the Old and New Testaments to be the verbally inspired Word of God, the final authority for faith and life, inerrant in the original writings, infallible, and God-breathed (2 Timothy 3:16,17; 2 Peter 1:20,21; Matthew 5:18; John 16:12,13).

Our Church, including myself, takes this view of the Bible. It is not just a view on our part, but it is the foundation for our faith and our authority for the way we live. We believe they are the true Words of God, hence verbally inspired.

By the authority, we mean it is what we look to for our measure for: salvation, right and wrong, decisions, and how we choose what is the right way to live, in general life.

We believe the Bible is inerrant in its original writings because we do believe humans were used by God to

190

write down His words. We do realize over the years some copies could have a typo or misspelling, but we hold to inerrancy in its originally manuscripts. Where the Bible is loud, I am loud; where the Bible is quiet, I am quiet. So the Bible is the basis for all we believe and all we proclaim.

I/we have faith that the Bible is truth and I/we believe it is truth because we believe its claim about itself to be the truth! (2 Timothy 3:16).

What a positive and unique way to communicate the fundamentals of the faith.

Struggles

Chris is open in sharing some of the difficulties Image Church has faced since its beginning. After moving into their new warehouse space, the church quickly shifted to a missional approach in the community. People began remodeling a shelter down the street from the church, people started bringing extra bags of food with them to the worship gatherings on Sundays, and the church saw more people committing their lives to Christ. All this was talking place just within the first few months of moving to a new facility. God was at work, but finances were tight.

The wonderful gift provided the meeting space. And the church was growing at a good rate—but the finances were not. Chris had seen many pastors who focused so much on money that they seemed to have lost sight of Who was their provider.

Chris shares from his own pain:

I struggled with how to lead in this. How do you ask people who have sacrificed to begin giving more? I couldn't do it. I quickly went to prayer, and God gave me the strength and the words to talk about money. We still face tight financial times, but God has always taken care of us. I realize, especially right now, everyone is going through this. But being a pastor and planting a church in an area where everything seems to be ten times more expensive does not help. So finances have been a blessing and a struggle.

Although the finances were an issue that needed to be addressed and taught, Chris struggled with another issue. He writes,

But I believe my greatest struggle was not leading as boldly and strongly as I needed to early on. This had nothing to do with money. I didn't know how to handle other leaders in our church. I should have used more candor, been more up front with people about what is expected of leadership, called people out immediately if they were not leading, and I should have just been more straight up with other leaders.

Significance

In August 2007, Chris wrote the following that illustrates the impact of Image Church:

Imagine a group of people giving all they can for the Kingdom, because they realize all they are and all they own comes from Jesus, because their hearts are exploding with gratitude, because they sacrifice for what they believe in, because they just can't help themselves … this is the church!

He continues to describe a night to celebrate baptism,

Image Church gathering took a different approach last night. We were truly a church without walls. We gathered outside by the pool for burgers and dogs, volleyball, horseshoes, swimming and, of course, a great time of worship under the open skies. Praise God for holding off the rain until it was over. I was a little concerned, after I arrived and realized that our entire church was showing up. Now this is not a negative, but I had not thought about parking, there were cars everywhere, I guess that is a good problem to have. What a great night! The highlight, of course, was baptizing three people who have decided to follow Jesus Christ!

Summary

Chris has a heart for the church and for church planters. He sums up his thoughts:

> Pray hard. Stay in the Word so you can stay focused on preaching the WORD of God boldly. This leads people to become worshippers of God. Strive to love people as much as possible. Strive to serve those right where you live and live with them ... not above them ... not below them and definitely not away from them. Live the way Jesus lived, do what Jesus did, make disciples, and lead the church with which He has entrusted you.

Soul

Most people would say that the heartbeat of Image Church is the value of ministry as seen in their mission statement, *Centered in Worship*, *Cultivated through Community*, and *Committed to Service*.

Chris shares about the impression Image Church is making in the community:

> Most people would say that is a driving mark of Image, is our community. The way people love and are constantly inviting others into that community is evident.

> One of the real life stories I love sharing is about a woman who did not know Jesus. She started coming to our church because her husband and kids were coming. It was around January of 2008 when she first walked in and began regularly attending. I remember she and her

husband had more ink than Picasso and DaVinci put together. For those of you that don't know, they had tattoos.

Her husband had nailed some things down in his walk with Jesus, and her kids loved gathering with our church. The husband started getting involved with our band, using his D.J. skills for worship! She began to enjoy being there, but told her husband she hated the fact that she loved it.

One Sunday she approached me and told me that our donuts, and I quote, "sucked!" Before I could respond she quickly said, "I would not complain, unless I had a remedy," so she began baking pastries for our gathering … and this was a good thing. She is an accomplished chef. Now Image had begun to grow, and we were pushing 200. All of this was right at our two-year anniversary mark. I often say it is attributed to God that we have a place to actually gather on Sunday mornings, and we have homemade gourmet pastries. In any church planting book you read, you just can't go wrong with that combination.

This lady even began to help with bringing in food for the shelter, and serving every week somewhere within the Body. It was Easter Sunday 2008 where God put it all together, and it made all of this truly worth it. She committed her life to Jesus!

A few months later their teenage daughter committed her life to Jesus, and in the summer of 2008, I baptized her and her daughter together while the dad helped lead the way! She now continues to make pastries and heads up a part of our children's ministry. That one story makes all of the rest well worth it!

Statistics and Structure

Image Church currently has 250 members with three staff members. They are a nondenominational church that desires to cooperate with other churches in the area of missions and church planting.

Image Church was launched with financial underwriting from Calvary Road Baptist Church, Alexandria, Virginia, in the spring of 2006.

The church currently leases simple warehouse space where all services are held. They also support an orphanage in China through Manna Worldwide. They have a goal of planting a church in China. They currently support two missionaries and a local shelter.

The church is led by six elders who oversee major areas of ministry.

ABOUT THE CHURCH PLANTER—

Chris Rhodenhizer is founding and Lead Pastor of Image Church (www.imagechurch.com), an independent non-denominational church in Dumfries, Virginia. The vision of Image Church is a community of people reflecting the image of Christ.

Their mission is to see people lead lives of worship, live in community with other believers, and serve the church and the world by being and making disciples.

Pastor Rhodenhizer is a 1996 graduate of Liberty University in Lynchburg, Virginia (B.S., Religion). He was ordained at Calvary Road Baptist Church in 1998.

He regularly writes a blog, www.chrisrhodenhizer.wordpress.com.

Chris and his wife Krista have been married since 1999 and have four children; Madelyn (2001), Liam (2003), Ava (2005), and Koen (2007).

Chapter 14
Finishing the Task

"I live my life in such a way that every day I try to accomplish at least one thing that will outlive me and last for eternity. God has literally taken me to the ends of the earth and back, to see this vision realized."

- Vernon Brewer

Story

In May of 1985, my wife, Debi, and I went to Virginia Baptist Hospital to see a friend who was recovering from surgery. Just a few days earlier, Vernon Brewer had had surgery to remove a five-pound tumor that was attached to his heart and lungs. The doctors told him that if he had waited one more week, it would have been too late. As Debi and I walked into Vernon's room, his father, Fred, greeted us, gave us a quick update and allowed us the privilege of praying for Vernon as he lay there, motionless, consumed with pain.

Vernon served as Dean of Students of Liberty University. He was the first graduate of the same school. He was the husband of a wonderful wife. He was the father of three wonderful little girls. He was a man who loved Jesus and loved the work to which God had called him. He was a man who was loved by the student body of Liberty. Dr. Falwell had called the college family of 2,400 plus students, staff, and faculty to a day of prayer and fasting to ask God for a miracle of Vernon's healing.

Vernon learned lessons of great vision, great hope, and great faith through the experiences of his life and through the example of his mentor, Jerry Falwell. At this point in this life, all seemed lost. He was told that survival was a long shot—and if he did survive, continuing the lifestyle that he had loved would be a miracle.

Vernon wrote in his own journal,

God, I've encouraged and prayed with others in times of crisis and tried to give them hope by reading the Bible. But this is different … it's me.

It's one thing to put my arm around someone and pray with them; it's quite another matter to cope with this overwhelming crisis in my own life. It's so hard. I feel like I'm drowning. All I can do is reach for You.[52]

He did reach for God—and as only He can do, God healed.

Vernon's experience with cancer served as a catalyst that would form and establish one of the largest church planting movements and support organizations in the world.

Founded in 1991 as a nonprofit, nondenominational Christian organization, World Help was developed as a uniquely qualified and strategic organization to use the people and resources so abundant in the West and take them to areas of the world where the need is most desperate. World Help exists to fulfill the Great Commission and the Great Commandment through partnering, training, helping, and serving, especially in the unreached areas of the world.[53]

In reviewing his life, Vernon has identified many times in his life as "defining moments," moments that clarify why God is doing what He is doing and often clarify *what* God is doing.

As a seventeen-year-old high school graduate, Vernon was asked by his uncle, Roscoe Brewer, to go on a youth mission trip to a little village

---

52   Vernon Brewer, *Why? Answers to Weather the Storms of Life* (WH Press, 2006), page 21.

53   www.worldhelp.net, Homepage and About Us.

in Mexico. Their task for the week was to construct a church building in a remote area where there was no church of any kind.[54]

When they had arrived, the foundation for the church that would hold approximately 300 people had already been laid by the missionaries in the area. During the cooler morning hours, the group would lay concrete block, mix cement, erect walls, and work on the roof. By week's end, they were whitewashing the exterior of the building, running simple electrical wiring, and stringing lights.

It was a simple building—but it was special building to the several hundred who would be coming to worship from the surrounding villages. They began work on Monday morning, and by Friday evening, they were ready to invite the surrounding villagers to come and dedicate the building.

During the construction process, afternoon temperatures soared too high for work. Instead, the youth mission's team would go to each village and hand out Spanish New Testaments.

In preparation for the afternoon distribution, Vernon needed to learn a simple phrase; in fact, just three words: *Regalo ... gratis ... suyo.* In Spanish, it meant, "Free gift for you".

> Vernon writes,
>
> I remember the dirt roads with open sewage running in front of houses and children playing outside the dilapidated shacks. Many wore no clothes. It was the worst poverty I had ever seen, the worst smells I had ever smelled. I was completely out of my comfort zone— confronted with great human need. I was emotionally drained and stretched beyond my limits.[55]
>
> As he called on the shacks that the people knew as home, he would say his three words, "Regalo gratis suyo," and hand each person a New Testament. The response was overwhelming: their eyes would light up,

---

54 Vernon Brewer, *Defining Moments, A Journey to the Ends of the Earth and Back* (WH Press, 2008), page 16.

55 Ibid, page 18

some would cry, some would hug their Bibles, some would even kiss their visitor.

The gift of new life through the presentation of a small Bible touched the lives of many villagers—but the experience of seeing lives changed touched a seventeen-year-old high school graduate. Vernon later writes,

> I don't think it's any coincidence that now, many years later, I'm still traveling the world, facilitating construction of modest village church buildings, and distributing "free gifts" to people who have never owned a Bible.
>
> Little did I know, as a 17-year-old young man, God was preparing me for what He wanted me to do with the rest of my life? I thought it would just be a fun youth trip to another country, but God used it to change the direction in my life.[56]

That was defining moment number one. I recently sat with Vernon, and he told me about defining moment number two.

In March of 1996, Liberty University leaders Wes Tuttle and Rob Jackson asked Vernon to come to India to dedicate a church that students had raised $4,000 to build and did so with their own hands.

After traveling for almost forty hours, Vernon arrived in New Delhi, a city of over eleven million people. The poverty, the smells, the hopelessness, and the starvation were heartbreaking. This, compounded by the spiritual domination and oppression, were overwhelming.

From New Delhi, they took a seven-hour train ride to a remote part of Rajasthan, home of the maharajas. Then a six-hour jeep ride to a small town that would end their day almost to their destination.

The next morning, Vernon accompanied a small team to a remote village about an hour from their night's stay. Karpina was where they would dedicate the new church. He was told that there was not another church within a fifty-mile radius in any direction. As they began,

---

56   Ibid, Page 19

Vernon was introduced to a young Indian pastor who had discipled 192 believers in a little more than a year. They had been meeting under a tree—and the new church building would be a place for worship, a place of fellowship, and a place of hope.

It was 9 a.m. Hundreds had already arrived to witness this phenomenon. Some walked, some rode bicycles, some came from as far as twenty miles.

As Vernon waited, another young pastor came to him with a stirring comment: He said that they had 1,000 pastors trained and ready to plant 1,000 new churches. He said all they needed was help.

That rocked Vernon to his soul. As he left the U.S. to come on this trip, he asked God to break his heart over the things that broke God's heart. It was happening.

Vernon writes,

> "It was then that I heard the still small voice of God saying, "Vernon, this is why I brought you to India. This is why I spared your life from cancer and gave you a new lease on life. This is why World Help was started. This is what I want you to do for the rest of your life—plant churches where no church exists."[57]

He quickly began to analyze and see what the cost of such an endeavor would be. Each church would cost $4,000 ... 1,000 trained pastors to lead these churches ... $4 million. He soon felt that proverbial hollow pit in his stomach and prayed silently, "God, I can't do this. It's too big!" He writes, "Once again, I heard that still small voice of God say, 'Good ... I can!'"[58]

As he went home, excited at what God had shown him and approved in him, Vernon began to tell others about his vision and the next project. Many tried to change his mind, many looked on in unbelief, and some even laughed.

---

57 Ibid, Page 117
58 Ibid, Page 117.

John Maxwell has often said, "If you tell someone your vision and they don't laugh, it's not big enough."

This one was big enough. It was a big need, it was a big goal, and it would take a big God!

As Vernon shared what God had revealed with his wife, Patti, they knew that they would have to lead by example. They quickly sold a car they had just purchased and used $1,000 to plant the first church.

Building 4,000 churches in India was appropriately named "Project Vision." Project Vision was completed by December 31, 1999.

On that New Year's Eve, World Help was still ten churches short of completing the project. As Vernon sat at home praying for God to do what only He could do, the phone rang. Someone on the other end, unknown to Vernon or World Help, was calling to announce that he was mailing a check for $40,000 to build ten new churches. As Vernon looked at his watch, it was 1:27 p.m., in the afternoon. He began to rejoice that God was early in answering his prayers. As he watched CNN bring in the new millennium around the world, he realized that India had an unusual time difference from the eastern coast of America; they were actually ten and a half hours ahead. The gift arrived right on time for India.

Vernon once told me, "It is not just about building church buildings but building churches, and it's not just about building churches but birthing a movement to reach a world for Christ!"

To date, World Help has been able to plant more than 42,000 churches, provide over 1,200 church buildings, and train over 29,000 church planters, pastors, and lay workers.

Strategy

World Help exists to fulfill the Great Commission and the Great Commandment through partnering, training, helping, and serving, especially in the unreached areas of the world.

Their most recent strategy, "one for one," is a missional plan designed to plant churches in villages and communities around the world. This "village transformation" strategy merges the efforts of humanitarian aid projects and child advocacy programs, combining both physical and spiritual help, leading to the real transformation of entire villages and communities.

They have established "core values" for their ministry that filter the strategy of this project.

- Authentic Relationships and Teamwork

- Fanatical Attention to Quality and Detail

- Working with Passion and Enthusiasm

- Always Doing What is Right

- Accomplishing God-Sized Tasks that will Last for Eternity[59]

This strategy begins with a *Missional Engagement* of partnership which is simple, intentional, and delivers hope and help.

It begins with *National Partners*. Nationals can go where Westerners can't, speak the languages Westerners don't know, and be a part of a culture where Westerners would be an outsider. Forming partnerships with Christian leaders native to the different areas helps break down cultural barriers and promotes openness and acceptance among those we are trying to reach.

It continues by *Equipping and Training the Missional Messenger*. Missional Messengers are trained and resourced by national partners to plant churches in least-reached villages and communities. This training is comprehensive and focuses on developing healthy spiritual leaders.

It requires that they *Go and Assess*. These messengers go to specific villages to assess how to best provide for both spiritual and physical needs.

---

59   www.worldhelp.net, Mission Statement.

World Help then *Combines Spiritual Hope with Humanitarian Aid*. Each village is distinct, and each messenger has the flexibility to find the best methods adapted for a particular culture.

Finally, they *Establish the House Church*. The messenger plants a house church in the homes of the first Christ followers of the village, allowing spiritual roots to take hold.[60]

Successes

Planting churches in South America, India, Russia, China, Vietnam, Cambodia, Africa, and other parts of the world through national partners and their strategies continues to expand the impact of World Help.

In addition, World Help has provided more than 8 million Bibles, New Testaments, and other pieces of Christian literature to public schools, churches, hospitals, military bases, and orphanages in countries such as Iraq, North Korea, Russia, China, India, Nepal, Myanmar, Vietnam, Laos, Rwanda, Haiti, the Philippines, and Cuba.[61]

Begun in 2000, the Children of the World choir has provided children with the opportunity to travel, raise child sponsorships, and promote the urgency of reaching the millions of children throughout the world who are in need or in danger every single day. Through the Children of the World's ten-month tour, the choir raises funds to provide new children's homes or refurbish existing facilities that provide care and shelter for thousands of needy children around the world. Also, each child in the choir is provided with a college scholarship in order to receive a quality education in preparation for the future ministry.[62]

Struggles

The greatest and most captivating struggles have focused on finding the right man for the right job. It becomes very easy for the Western church to pacify their desire to reach the world through unproved and

---

60   *Project oneforone: a global church-planting initiative*; World Help, page 3.
61   www.worldhelp.net, Bible Distribution
62   Ibid, Children of the World

untested missions programs. World Help has often been moved by the "compassion" of a potential national partner. Adherence to the core values of World Help and consistency with the principles of Scripture must be foundational.

The greatest struggle has been to find leadership among nationals in the target culture who will embrace the ministry values of World Help and operationally incorporate those values into the infrastructure of the national organization.

Significance

Vernon Brewer was deeply impacted by the ministry, vision, and calling of Jerry Falwell. He was the first graduate of Lynchburg Baptist College, now Liberty University. He served as the Dean of Students and as a Vice President of the University.

> Jonathan Falwell recently wrote,
>
> Dad worked closely with Vernon as through the years they jointly sought new ways to reach the world for Christ. I had the great privilege of traveling with both of them to the far corners of this world in pursuit of this noble effort. It was through these travels, as well as God's calling on my life, that I began to see the importance of having a global vision—rather than just a local vision.
>
> Recently, I was talking to Dr. Elmer Towns, the co-founder of Liberty University, about my father's heaven-inspired vision. Elmer shared a few words in that conversation that will forever be emblazoned on my heart. He said, "Your dad was probably the only person I ever met who had a great desire to reach the world for Christ, and was actually crazy enough to believe that he could do it." In my estimation, Vernon Brewer is in that same category. Like my father, he has an audacious, almost fearless, faith.[63]

---

63   Ibid, Introduction.

Although impacted by the vision of faith of Dr. Falwell in a different manner from other church planters, Vernon captured the essence of reaching the world for Christ though the planting of churches where no church exists.

His vision not only continues through the ministry of World Help, but also through his desire to encourage churches to engage in "simultaneous impact," both locally and globally in reaching their Jerusalem, AND their Judea, their Samaria, AND even to the uttermost parts of the earth.

Summary

"Simultaneous impact" is the challenge that every local church, newly planted or established, faces. The ability to create a continuous world "touch" locally and globally defines the scope of a body's outreach to the world.

Vernon tells the story of a young church planter who established a work just outside of Atlanta. This young pastor asked World Help to come and help communicate the need to reach a world for Christ.

The church plant was young, only one or two years old at the time, and was still using a rented facility each week as they set up their portable worship center. They had, though, begun raising money to buy and build a facility. In their relocation fund was $4,000.

As Vernon shared his heart and began to talk about reaching this world for Christ through planting other churches, using national pastors, in places where no church existed, Pastor Brian Bloye began to sense the prompting of God to respond in a most unusual way.

At the conclusion, Pastor Brian candidly told the young congregation of West Ridge Church that God was prompting him to help build a church where no church existed—not in Atlanta but in another part of the world, partnering with World Help and their network of national pastors.

West Ridge Church presented World Help with $4,000 from their own building fund and built a church on the other side of the world—and birthed a movement.

Brewer feels there is a biblical principle in a missional approach to world outreach as illustrated by a threefold cord being not easily broken (Ecclesiastes 4:12).

His three "strands" are identified as Framework, Formation, and Funding.

Framework is seen as the necessity to having the proper national partner. This is critical to developing the correct strategy. In many cultures, the first step in the process of impacting an area is to identify the "man of peace." The national partner helps identify the man of peace and ensures that he has the proper calling and anointing to engage in this work.

Formation is the facilitating partnership between the national partner and World Help. World Help begins the "vetting" process to determine the viability of the national partner and their experience in reaching the objectives necessary to impact the culture. This formation may occur over a lengthy period of time, sharing one project at a time, to develop the needed competencies and skills for ongoing programs.

Funding is the third strand of this threefold cord. Funding is the introductory process of World Help communicating and sourcing the opportunities to various donors and local churches. This begins the process of building authentic relationships between the national partner and the local church.

Soul

The soul of World Help is the opportunity to partner with national partners and local donors and churches to reach the world for Christ. It is the threefold cord of Framework, Formation, and Funding.

Statistics and Structure

Founded in 1991, to date World Help has:

- Established partnerships in over 60 countries.

- Planted over 43,000 new churches through their national partners.

- Constructed more than 1,200 new church buildings.

- Trained over 32,000 national church pastoral leaders.

- Cultivated an estimated 4 million new Christ-followers.

- Distributed more than $88 million in humanitarian aid.

- Provided nearly 9 million Bibles.

- Given care to more than 31,000 children through child sponsorships.

World Help is supported through the contributions and gifts of supporters throughout the world.

World help is a 501 (c) 3 registered not-for-profit organization providing aid to the soul and to the person. They are governed by a board of directors. They are also a recognized member of ECFA.

"I am at the place in my life where I want to leave a legacy. Every day I try to accomplish at least one thing that will outlive me and last for eternity and I can't think of a better legacy to leave than planting a church where no church exists."

- Vernon Brewer
President, World Help

ABOUT THE CHURCH PLANTER—

Vernon Brewer is the founder and President of World Help, a nonprofit, non-denominational Christian organization that was founded to meet the spiritual and physical needs of hurting people around the world.

Vernon is also author of *The Forgotten Children: Hungry. Hopeless. Running for their lives.; Why? Answers to Weather the Storms of Life; Children of Hope: Be touched. Be inspired. Be changed; and Defining Moments: A Journey to the Ends of the Earth and Back.*

Vernon has conducted international evangelistic campaigns and rallies in more than fifty foreign countries worldwide, as well as numerous leadership training conferences in Uganda, China, India, Nepal, Burma, Romania, and Russia. In addition, he has personally taken over 4,000 people to the mission field. He has led over 500 local church evangelistic rallies, and has lectured on 30 college and university campuses. He has spoken to over 1 million teenagers in public high school assembly programs and is a frequent speaker at camps and conferences.

Vernon lives with his wife, Patti, and his son, Josh, in Forest, Virginia. He has three married daughters and four grandsons.

Chapter 15
A Church-Planting Movement Is Born: The Liberty Center for Church Planting

Guest Chapter by Dr. Dave Earley

"God is birthing church planting movements all over the world. It is exciting to see Him creating a river of fearless church planters who are willing to risk; who are not satisfied unless they have turned the world upside down; who will take the Gospel to the people who are dying to hear it."

- Dr. Dave Earley

Story

In 1979 God called me, a twenty-year-old college student, to plant a church with a team. Six years later, I led of team of four young men and their wives to Columbus, Ohio, to launch a new church. We moved knowing that we had no building and no budget. We only had a handful of people interested in the new church—eleven adults and a baby. But we had something every church must have: a vision and commitment to launch the most biblical, Spirit-led, healthy and evangelistic church we could.

Our first month in Ohio, we met nightly for one hour of corporate prayer for jobs and the new church.

The second month we began to advertise and knocked on 400 doors in the community, taking a church interest survey. At the end of the second month, we went public in the music room at a middle school and were thrilled when fifty-four local people joined us.

We grew every week for the next year and a half to an attendance of over 200. Our church grew every year for the first twenty years of our existence until our average attendance was nearly 2,000, with more than 100 small groups for adults and teens, 66 acres of property, 70 percent of our members in ministry, and over 100 people baptized annually. We also had planted four daughter churches and had several others on the way. Our goal was to start twenty new churches by the year 2020.

My last years in Ohio, I realized that our single church, at best, would be able to train and send only one church planter and church planting team a year. During this time, Dr. Ergun Caner, of Liberty Baptist Theological Seminary, contacted me about starting a Center for Church Planting as part of Dr. Jerry Falwell's vision of planting 500 new churches. After much prayer, I agreed that this was a very strategic opportunity. I changed my doctoral dissertation to focus on what it would take to start a Center for Church Planting at Liberty.

In June of 2006, I moved to Lynchburg, Virginia, and took on the role as associate professor of pastoral leadership for Liberty Baptist Theological Seminary and head of the Center for Ministry Training, of which church planting was to become a part.

The Liberty Center for Church Planting was born July 1, 2006, when Dr. David Wheeler and I came on board, determined to again put Liberty on the map as the school that focuses on training church planters. That week, Dr. Jerry Falwell and Dr. Ergun Caner of Liberty along with Dr. Richard Harris of the North American Mission Board and Geoff Hammond of the Southern Baptist Conservatives of Virginia signed an agreement making Dr. Wheeler the official Southern Baptist field representative on the campus of Liberty. Dr. Wheeler's expertise in recruiting students and in applied servant evangelism turned out to be a great fit for church planting training.

However, our initial enthusiasm waned when no seminary students signed up to take the basic course in church planting. But my doctoral dissertation had a nine-step plan, and we began to follow it. As a result of the blessing of God on our efforts, the number of churches planted through the Liberty Center for Church Planting has gone from 10 in 2006, to 21 in 2007, to 40 in 2008. By the grace of God, we have helped spark a church-planting movement. Starting a church-planting movement is like starting a church. We need to wisely work as though it all depends upon us and pray as though it all depends upon God.

Strategy

The Nine-Step Plan for Creating a Center for Church Planting

As with any plan, we have made some adjustments along the way, but for the most part we have followed the plan that I put together as part of my doctoral studies. A brief look at the plan and how it has worked out up until this point reveals how God has seen fit to bless this process.

1. Create a Master of Arts in Church Planting

Realizing that Liberty was becoming the largest and fastest growing online seminary in the world, we worked through the process of academic bureaucracy to develop three new courses and create a 36 credit hour MA in church planting.

The new classes (Methods, Models, Context and Culture; Strategic Prayer and Spiritual Warfare; and Leading a Healthy Church), were developed out of the research from my doctoral dissertation. This new degree was instantly very popular and had over 200 students enrolled within the first two years. This short, simple MA also made it easier for us to recruit Liberty grads to spend their first year out of college completing an MA in church planting residentially at our seminary.

2. Create an MDiv Concentration in Church Planting

The next step was plugging into the existing Master of Divinity the church planting core classes already developed for the MA in church planting. This also became a popular selection for many students.

3. Create a Church-Planting Presence on the Campus of Liberty University

Liberty University, with over 10,000 undergraduate students, and Liberty Baptist Seminary, with several hundred students, seemingly had huge potential to provide the planters needed to create a church-planting movement. Yet only a handful of students were actively considering church planting. The goal was to put church planting on the radar for the students of Liberty University and Liberty Theological Seminary. We took several steps to make this happen:

a. Church Planter Get-Togethers

Most students like to get off campus and are curious about their professors. So we began to hold monthly church-planting get-togethers at my house. Dr. Rod Dempsey, Dr. Wheeler, and I would personally invite students to come. Soon we were having forty to fifty students show up to eat pizza, hear a church planter tell his story, and ask questions.

b. Taste and See Events

The goal was to get as many interested students as possible to taste and see what church planting is all about. We worked with John Bailey and Steve Canter of NAMB to hold a Friday night event in which students sat around tables and, in the course of four hours, ate pizza, got to know each other, and were guided to strategize how they'd plant a church in a strategic city.

c. Position Church Planting as part of the Annual Undergraduate Missions Emphasis Week

The idea was to get church planting to be considered part of the annual missions emphasis week, yet the doors were not opening to make this happen. Then in the summer of 2007 Jonathan Falwell assumed the role of senior pastor of Thomas Road Baptist Church with the passion to fulfill his father's vision of planting 500 churches. With his help, we created a Church Planting Emphasis Week for Liberty University at the end of January 2008. Between convocation, which is attended by 7,000 students; campus church; an internship fair; and guest speakers in various classes, we touched a large section of the student body. This put church planting on the radar of our undergraduate students. Now we have been allowed to hold two such emphases each school year.

d. Have an Annual Church Planting Chapel in the Undergraduate Ministry Chapel.

As the director of the Center for Ministry Training, I was given responsibility for Ministry Chapel. We began to schedule church planters to speak as often as once a month.

4. Create a National Newsletter

Our first few months we worked hard to mine the Liberty student family and developed a mailing list of over a thousand religion students, seminary students, faculty members, graduates, and churches. We then created two newsletters, one sharing all the activities of the Center for Ministry Training, and the other the ministries of the Center for Church Planting. In the church planting newsletter, we told the story of a different Liberty church planter in each issue. These articles became very popular.

5. Position Church Planting as part of the Annual Super Conference Week

Thomas Road Baptist Church has long held an annual pastors' conference called Super Conference. In 2008, Jonathan Falwell made church planting the focus of the last half day of the conference. This greatly increased the profile of what we were trying to accomplish nationally. It has helped us recruit students into our online MA in Church Planting.

6. Use the World Wide Web to Recruit

Again TRBC helped us as they developed a national website, www. innovatechurch.us in 2008. The editor, Matt Wilmington, is careful to feature church planters and church planting frequently on the website.

7. Network

Many people were already doing significant work in church planting. Our goal was to discover and develop relationships. As expected, because of the nature of church planting, most church-planting leaders are very helpful to any cause that aids church planting. Since our primary role is recruiting and training, we have been able to develop strategic partnerships with various solid church-planting organizations to assess, fund, and coach our church planters after they are on the field.

8. Positively Influence the Liberty Baptist Fellowship for Church Planting

The Liberty Baptist Fellowship was started by Dr. Jerry Falwell in 1980 as a fellowship of churches/pastors organized to plant local "baptistic" churches. Since then, over 200 churches have been started, and several new church planters are currently being supported. In December of 2006, after pastoring for thirty-plus years, Dr. Leland (Lee) Dittman became the first full-time director of Liberty Baptist Fellowship. By having a fulltime director, LBF has been able to grow and adapt to the needs of the twenty-first century.

> In 2005, I wrote,
>
> The LBF needs to separate the Chaplaincy section from the Church Planting section. The Board should be restructured so that it represents more progressive, missional thinkers. It can be used as a means of assessing, training, funding, networking, and coaching non-Southern Baptist church planters. It would also provide a place where non-Southern Baptist Liberty

alumni pastors and Super Conference participants can
give back to the school.

Today, I am happy to say, under the leadership of Dr. Dittman, the
LBF has made all of these adjustments. They have been our primary
partner in providing funding to our church planters and the Center for
Church Planting.

9. Pray

In 2005 I wrote,

> [Prayer] is not mentioned last because it is least
> important; rather it is the most important. God is
> the church builder. He is more than able and willing
> to guide and provide all that is needed to build His
> church and advance His kingdom. Church planting is
> an inexact science and a spiritual activity. The mighty
> resource of prayer must not be neglected. The parts of
> the world exploding in church planting (Nigeria, Korea,
> South America) have done so out of the overflow of
> a prayer movement. The author believes that God is
> leading him to Liberty Theological Seminary to help
> kindle/rekindle a renewed move of God in prayer.

After a year of serving at Liberty, I realized that I did not have the
time and energy to do all I was responsible to do, plus start a church-
planting movement, *and* launch a prayer movement. Fortunately, at
this time, God sent Daniel Henderson to Liberty Baptist Theological
Seminary to launch a prayer movement as part of his Strategic Renewal
ministry. Since then, we have tried to partner with Strategic Renewal as
much as possible in order to promote prayer in the lives of our students
and on the campus of Liberty University.

Summary

Our sovereign Savior loves the church and gave Himself for it. He
promised to build His church, and the gates of hell cannot prevail
against it. God is birthing church-planting movements all over the

world. It is exciting to see Him creating a river of fearless church planters who are willing to risk; who are not satisfied unless they have turned the world upside down; who will take the Gospel to the people who are dying to hear it.

ABOUT THE CHURCH PLANTER—

Dr. Dave Earley (www.daveearley.net) is an experienced church planter and coach.

He serves as the Director of the Liberty Center for Church Planting at Liberty Theological Seminary. He is also Chairman of the Department of Pastoral Leadership and Church Planting for Liberty Theological Seminary.

He has authored twelve books on subjects such as small groups, leadership, prayer, and the Christian life.

Chapter 16
Liberty Baptist Fellowship

Guest chapter by Dr. Leland (Lee) Dittman

"We do not just want to hold services and construct buildings, we want to aggressively preach the Gospel to lost people and capture towns for Christ."

- Dr. Jerry Falwell, 1981

Story

Liberty Baptist Fellowship was born in the heart of Dr. Jerry Falwell. He saw that, for the most part, old, established churches were complacent and had stopped reaching their areas for Christ. In the *Liberty Journal* for September 1981, Dr. Falwell stated,

> Unfortunately, many of our conservative churches represent little more than dead orthodoxy. They believe the right things but their practical evangelism is nil ... When a church is not aggressively winning people to Christ, it will become introspective and introverted until it is isolated from any real influence in the community. In time it will virtually die.

Dr. Falwell not only pointed out the problem with the existing church but also presented a solution. In that same issue of the *Journal*, Dr. Falwell announced the creation of the Liberty Baptist Fellowship under the title "New Fellowship will Plant Churches." In the article, he said,

Liberty Baptist Fellowship is a network of "like-minded and like-practice" churches that will encourage church planting through education, advertisement, and stimulation. This will take the form of seminars, national conferences, a national newspaper and organizational manuals. The foundational plank in the fellowship is "Churches plant churches," so the fellowship will help churches plant churches.

Dr. Falwell went on to write,

> We want to build fundamentalist churches, which means they are committed to the conservative doctrines of Christianity which include the authority of the Word of God. And we are a fellowship of churches that will rigorously defend those doctrines. Next our churches will display super aggressive evangelism. We do not just want to hold services and construct buildings, we want to aggressively preach the Gospel to lost people and capture towns for Christ. This means we will preach, teach and disciple as many people as possible.

Down through the years our purpose has not changed.

On October 20, 1981, at 2 p.m. in the sanctuary of Thomas Road Baptist Church, the Liberty Baptist Fellowship was formally organized to plant new churches that are "baptistic" in doctrine and practice and aggressively evangelistic. The fellowship was formed with its own board of directors and Dr. Rudy Holland serving as the first president.

By 1982, the fellowship was approached by graduates of the seminary who had a desire to become chaplains. They needed to be endorsed by a denomination or fellowship of churches. The LBF applied and was approved by the Armed Forces Chaplains Board as an official endorsing agency. Dr. Elmer Towns became LBF's first endorsing agent. Forty-five chaplains are presently endorsed through the LBF. Dr. Charles Davidson, who recently retired as a Lieutenant Colonel in the Air Force chaplaincy, is our current endorser.

From its inception in September 1981 to November 2006, the fellowship was staffed with volunteers. God used these dedicated men to plant over 300 churches in those twenty-five years. We could not do what we are doing today without the work of these dedicated servants of God. In 2006, the board discerned the need to increase our effectiveness by hiring a full-time director. They voted in September of 2006 to call this writer as the first full-time Director of the fellowship. I had attended Lynchburg Baptist College (LU) and had been a pastor for thirty years. I had also planted my own church in Cedar Brook, New Jersey, in 1978, which started with twelve individuals and grew to 450 in two years. I served on the board of directors for LBF for ten years and had been president of the board for six years.

With a new director in place, Dr. Falwell realized that we would need to increase the amount of money the fellowship raised to plant more churches. To facilitate this, he created a partnership between Liberty University and the LBF. In an article in the *Journal* entitled "Partnering in Church Planting," Dr. Falwell, the executive chairman of the fellowship, approved three benefits for pastors joining the LBF. First, all full-time pastors are eligible to receive a tuition-free scholarship to any of Liberty Univsersity's Distance Learning Programs (DLP), excluding the PhD. Second, all new resident students attending Liberty University from LBF churches may be able to receive a $1,000 scholarship annually for four years. Third, LBF pastors are allowed to register for the Super Conference free.

Needless to say, we had an overwhelming response. Within a year we went from 150 churches supporting the fellowship to over 1,000. Our funding for church planting efforts went from $50,000 per year to $800,000, which allowed us to increase the number of church plants from five each year to planting more than thirty.

Strategy and Structure

Church planters who desire to partner with LBF must first fill out an application. This application contains: personal information about the planter and his family; an authorization to do background checks; a request for demographics of the area where he wants to plant the church; his doctrinal positions on such issues as the Godhead, salvation, etc.; educational background; personal budget; church plant budget; giving record over the last year; a copy of his ordination; a copy of his transcripts; a picture of him and his family; and four recommendation forms to be filled out by four people who know him well.

When all this material is received in our office, we check out the references and other material. When satisfied that everything is in place, we set up an interview with two members of our board of directors during one of our four yearly meetings. If the interviewers recommend the candidate, the board votes on supporting him for the next year. Church planters can find the application and forms on our website, www.libertybaptistfellowship.com.

Our support at the present consists of $1,000 per month for the planter for twelve months. This support starts thirty days after they launch their new church. The thirty-day rule was applied because of some problems we had in the first few years of LBF. Originally we had started supporting a planter immediately, even though he might not be ready to launch for six or seven months. We soon realized we had to change our policy. We had cases where we gave the support to several individuals who decided after receiving several months of support that they no longer desired to be church planters. Wanting to use God's money wisely, we imposed the thirty-day rule.

Along with support, we assign one of our board members as a mentor to the planter. He is there to help when questions arise or to offer other support. We have given planters communion sets, books, and other material they might need. Once the church plant is launched, we ask the church planter to put LBF on the mission budget so that we can continue to invest that money in new churches.

Our board is meeting this month to discuss some changes in support for church planters. Some of the ideas we are considering are giving a church planter $2,000 per month for twelve months and then have them start to repay that amount on the thirteenth month at $500 per month or 10 percent of their offerings, whichever is more, until the $24,000 is paid back. After that we are asking them to put LBF on as a mission outreach at the rate of 2 percent of their offerings.

A second proposal would be to have the church planter raise $30,000, and we would match that amount as start-up money. Then we would make up the difference between their monthly offerings and $7,500 for the first six months, up to a total of $20,000. On the seventh month, the church would begin to repay that amount at $800 or 10 percent of their offerings a month, whichever is greater, until the total amount is paid back. Then we would ask them to put us on their mission budget for 2 percent of their offerings so we could reinvest that money in church planting.

We would most likely also offer our present support of $1,000 per month for twelve months, but have the church planter begin to pay back that amount on the thirteenth month at $500 or 10 percent of their offerings, whichever is greater, and, when the amount is paid back, put LBF on their missions budget for 2 percent of their offerings.

We are also going to require all future planters to go through an assessment at the Seminary to ascertain their ability to pastor a church plant. Any future church planter will have to have a team of at least thirty in place and also have a worship leader on staff. We have found down through the years that these things are necessary to have a successful church launch.

Successes

We have had many successful church plants in the last twenty-seven years, such as David Rhodenhizer who planted Calvary Road Baptist Church in Alexandria, Virginia (see chapter 3); Daniel Henderson and Seacoma Community Baptist Church in Kent, Washington; Ken Hankins, who planted Seven Lakes Baptist Church in Seven Lakes, North Carolina; and Roscoe Lilly and North Star Church in Clifton Park, New York. If we were to list all of the churches that have succeeded and are averaging several hundred in attendance today, Dr. Miller's book would not have enough room to contain the stories. But there are a few stories that really stand out.

In 1985, Dave Earley put together a team to start a church in Gehanna, Ohio. Even though this area is not known as the Bible belt, and there were many obstacles to building a great church, Dave and his team went in with some fresh ideas and planted New Life Community Church. With the help of Liberty Baptist Fellowship, the church grew to become one of the largest churches in that area, running several thousand per Sunday and started several other churches in that area. Dr. Earley is now the director of Church Planting here at Liberty Seminary.

In January 1998, Matt Fry came to us and presented his vision of planting Cleveland Community Church in North Carolina (see chapter 7). Matt had a real burden for that area and had great success the first year, averaging 200 to 300 in attendance. The church continued to grow, and Matt began to look for a new location that would hold the crowds that were attending. He decided to build a new building in Clayton, North Carolina, and rename it 3C church. They built a beautiful new complex, and soon they ran out of space, so they built an even bigger addition onto the existing structure. Today they have a beautiful complex, and they have over 5,000 in attendance on any given Sunday. They are now making plans to add another location in Raleigh, North Carolina, to accommodate the people who drive from Raleigh to Clayton each week.

Another great story is that of Steven Furtick. Steven presented his vision of Elevation Church to the board at the end of 2005. He wanted to build an aggressive contemporary church to reach young people for Christ in Charlotte, North Carolina. On his first anniversary, attendance was running over 1,000 per Sunday. They had made a goal of 3,000 on their second anniversary. On February 2008 they exceeded that number with over 4,000 in attendance. Today, Steven pastors a church with multiple locations, whose attendance averages several thousand per Sunday.

In 2003, Buz Offenbacker approached the fellowship with a vision of starting a church in Williamstown, New Jersey. The board bought into his vision, and Buz started Word Church in a school building. Since that time they have purchased 37 acres and have plans for a $3 million complex. On their fifth anniversary they had approximately to 800 in attendance.

Jimmy Carroll, now a member of the LBF board of directors, wanted to start a church in Raleigh, North Carolina (see chapter 11). Jimmy rented an old warehouse and renovated the interior. His church began to grow and today, Journey Church runs several hundred with a Saturday night service and two Sunday morning services. He recently started a satellite campus in north Raleigh.

Michael Lukaszewski felt led to plant Oak Leaf Church in Cartersville, Georgia. When he applied to the LBF, the board could sense the excitement and vision that he had to reach that area. He launched in March 2007, and today more than a thousand are attending his Sunday morning services. Michael, like most of our church planters, is also planting other churches out of his church. LBF does not want to just add churches; we want to multiply church plants to reach this nation for Christ.

Struggles

Planting a church is not an easy task. There will be times of loneliness and discouragement. I have talked often with one planter who started out with what he thought was a great team, only to find after six months that most of the team had different ideas about how to plant a church than he did. Soon the team members started leaving the work, and he became quite discouraged. One member of the team even took back the sound equipment he had purchased for the church plant. But God had called this young man to plant this church. In the next few months God brought in other people who caught the vision, and soon he was able to build a new team with men who were united behind his vision.

That is the reason church planting is a calling. Just as God lays it on the heart of an individual to go the mission field overseas, God calls people to plant churches in specific areas. If you were not called, you would soon quit. But if God has called you to plant a church, then He will go with you through every valley, will supply your needs, and will help you succeed.

Not only do you need to be called to be successful, you also need to begin with an assessment. This will determine your strengths and weaknesses. Once you find your weaknesses, you can find team members who are strong in those particular areas who will help you build the church. One person you will definitely need is a worship leader. Today there is such a great emphasis on worship that you must have this person in place when you launch if you want to reach this generation for Christ.

You need to raise start-up costs. It usually takes $60,000–70,000 to have a good launch. You will need sound equipment, advertisement, mailings, and hundreds of other things along with building rent. That is one reason that the board is considering matching up to $30,000 in start-up costs for our church plants. A strong launch will mean a successful first year.

Coaching is another important factor. Most church planters are new in the ministry. Even though they have been through seminary, there are so many things to learn that a good coach is imperative. LBF and Liberty Seminary will be working together to supply coaching for our church planters. We want our church planters to know that we are there to assist them in any way we can, especially during that crucial first year.

Most of all, you will need prayer. God is able to do exceedingly more than you can even envision. Don't get so caught up in ministry that you forget the One for whom you are doing it. If God has placed a call on your life to plant a church, you can be assured that He will help you fulfill your vision.

Soul and Significance

Jerry Falwell realized that our nation was not the Christian nation it once was. When you read the statistics that in 1900 there were 27 churches for every 10,000 people and today there are less then 11 churches per 100,000 people, you realize that we are going backwards. Add to this equation the fact that every major cultic group has targeted the United States as their mission field, you realize that instead of America being a mission sending country, we are in need of evangelizing. In America there are 323 million people, and 226 million of them are lost. We have become a mission field.

Did you know that the second largest Iranian city in the world is in the Los Angeles area, or that there are more Buddhists in the

U.S. than Episcopalians? Do you realize that Muslims now outnumber Presbyterians in the U.S., and they will soon outnumber American Jews? Our military has 10,000 Muslims, with three Muslim chaplains and eight more in training.

We are no longer the country that our forefathers founded on biblical principles. Christianity is declining, and other religions are filling the void. How can we turn things around? Dr. Falwell realized that the greatest evangelistic method under heaven is church planting. The answer is to plant evangelical churches in as many towns and cities as possible, to go right into the enemy's stronghold with the soul-saving Gospel.

New church plants are more evangelistic then established congregations. Bruce McNicol of Interest Ministries is quoted in *Christianity Today* as saying, "Among evangelical churches, those under three years old will win ten people to Christ per year for every hundred church members; those 3 to 15 years old will win five people per year. After age 15, the number drops to three per year."[64]

Older churches tend to be self-centered, looking for ways to minister to themselves. The culture of long-established churches is to care more for their members then they do for those who do not know Christ. One study found that 89 percent of church members believe that the church's main purpose is to take care of their own family. Only 11 percent said the main purpose of the church is to win the world for Jesus Christ. Usually a church reaches its peak in size during the first few decades of its existence. Then churches plateau in size and began to shrink in numbers, while all around them souls are stepping out into eternity lost. Mark Mitelberg expresses this in his book *Building a Contagious Church*: "the second law of spiritual dynamics warns us that all of us in the Christian community, left to ourselves, move toward spiritual self-centeredness."[65]

That was the impetus behind starting the LBF. Dr. Falwell saw the need and realized the lateness of the hour. In the September 1981 issue

---

64   Quoted in James P. Allen, "Why Plant a New Church?" (n.d.), http://www. rivervalleychristianchurch.com/pdf/why-plant.pdf, viewed April 25, 2009

65   Mark Mitelberg, *Building a Contagious Church* (Grand Rapids: Zondervan, 2002), p. 106.

of the *Liberty Journal* he wrote, "this organization (LBF) will be a tool to help reach the goal of beginning 5,000 new churches by the year 2000. We are banding together because we can do more together than any one [can] alone." Dr. Falwell realized that church planting was the best way to revive this country and reach the masses. This is still the driving force behind Liberty Baptist Fellowship today.

ABOUT THE CHURCH PLANTER—

Leland (Lee) Dittman attended Lynchburg Baptist College from 1975 to 1978.

He earned his master's degree from Luther Rice Seminary in Jacksonville, Florida, and his DMin from Antietam Biblical Seminary in Hagerstown, Maryland.

Lee planted his first church in New Jersey which grew from 12 to 450 in two years. He has also pastored four established churches in Pennsylvania, North Carolina, and New York. In April of 2006 he was called to be the first full-time director of Liberty Baptist Fellowship.

Lee and his wife Leni reside in Evington, Virginia.

Chapter 17
A Vision and a Strategy
for Church Planting

Guest chapter by Jonathan Falwell

"I truly believe church planting is the greatest avenue by which we can win souls to Christ. It must become our passion."

- Jonathan Falwell

Story

On a warm summer day in June 1956, a young man who had just graduated from Bible college arrived in his small hometown with a heaven-inspired vision to start a local church to reach his community with the Gospel of Christ. On the first day of this brand-new church plant, thirty-five adults and their children packed into Mountain View Elementary School in Lynchburg, Virginia—where the young pastor had once attended classes—to begin writing the story of a church that would reach far beyond the wildest dreams of anyone in that small southern town.

That young man's name was Jerry Falwell, my father. And although Dad's initial vision was to plant a local church much like the one he had been saved in four years earlier, God continually expanded the vision so that the church would ultimately have an astonishing and continuing worldwide impact. I'm not sure when the initial vision began to change, but it is undeniable that it didn't take long before Dad was looking far beyond surrounding neighborhoods and beginning to envision affecting the uttermost parts of the earth. Through Thomas Road Baptist Church, Liberty University, and related missions organizations, the seemingly insignificant congregation that met for the first time on that summer day in 1956 has gone on to be on the cutting edge of ministry and outreach and church innovation.

The church's early vision had a three-part structure:

1. God began to plant multiple visions for evangelism and Christian training in the heart of the young pastor who had an audacious, almost fearless, faith.

2. That pastor boldly followed God's call and continually illuminated the heaven-inspired plans to the congregation.

3. The congregation willingly joined in following the vision, often disregarding their personal comfort.

Strategy

Early in the history of Thomas Road Baptist Church, my father coined a phrase that has been at the very heart of TRBC and Liberty University throughout their histories. That phrase, "Saturation Evangelism," means: "Reaching every available person at every available time using every available means." This simple evangelism model was the plan of action that led Dad to begin a variety of (at the time) revolutionary approaches to evangelism.

After initiating a local radio program shortly after the church's launch, Dad soon was taking the Gospel to the television airwaves on the local ABC station WLVA (now WSET), even though some saw this as ridiculous. Later, God would reveal to Dad how television could have a national and international application for spreading the Gospel. It was also during this early phase of his ministry that Dad continued to reach out to Lynchburg and surrounding areas. In fact, he rose early every morning to knock on at least 100 doors in the Lynchburg community every day, six days a week. You see, not only did he have a vision, he had a passion. And without passion, the vision will certainly die.

Dad often said that many people were not home when he visited. For them he would leave a card with details about the new church. For those who were home, he would tell how he wanted to be a pastor who was available to them, no matter what their needs. Dad was extraordinarily determined in those days that by knocking on doors he would capture his hometown for Christ. And that little church that had started with thirty-five adults grew to nearly 900 on its first anniversary. There was no denying that God was at work in the church that was meeting in a converted Donald Duck bottling plant. The rest of the story of TRBC is one that many have studied as a model of church growth.

In the midst of shepherding that young local church, Dad began to experience another vision within his heart. This new vision of church planting was one that would impact many other communities just like Lynchburg. Dad knew that if he was going to fulfill the mission statement given in Acts 1:8, he would need to expand the borders of his vision well beyond the confines of his modest hometown. And he would need to encourage other church planters like himself to go and do likewise.

The church-planting dream would come to be fulfilled through education. A few years after the initial vision for massive church-planting projects, Thomas Road Baptist Church sponsored the creation of Lynchburg Christian Academy (preschool-12 education system), which was soon followed by the founding of Liberty University (originally Lynchburg Baptist College). As the years progressed, Liberty Baptist Theological Seminary, the Liberty University School of Law, and other innovative programs would be launched. Today, Liberty is the largest evangelical Christian college in America.

Initiating this Christian educational system was integral to carrying out the vision of global church planting that started in the late 1950s. Both educational entities have gone on to become institutions that serve as the necessary vehicle to send out godly and capable church planters, pastors, youth pastors, church leaders, missionaries and lay workers around the world with a passion for the local church.

On its website, 21st Century Strategies Inc. lists the "Top Mistakes in Church Planting," with number one being "Fast-tracking wrong people into leadership." That is another key component of Liberty University and Liberty Baptist Theological Seminary: we desire to train prayerful, humble, and qualified pastors to take on the important responsibility of leading new church plants. Sure, there will be failures, but we want to prepare our pastors as best we know how to be godly shepherds of their flocks.

Successes

At the onset of Liberty, Dad brought in Christian leaders to help him train new pastors. They included: Dr. Elmer Towns, Dr. Harold Willmington, Dr. Robert Hughes, and a handful of others who would help cast the vision for church planting and evangelism through the young school. Dad began saying often and loudly that he wanted Liberty to ultimately send out 5,000 church planters and 5,000 missionaries to cover the globe with the Gospel. I'm sure some thought such plans frivolous. But God had planted the vision, and Dad would not compromise it.

As a result, God honored that vision and throughout Dad's life he was able to see thousands of churches planted in cities all across America. Thousands of Liberty Christian Academy and Liberty University students have gone out from Lynchburg to get involved in local church and church-planting efforts with the desire of capturing their own towns for Christ. This was a vision that Dad was passionate about and one that still burns brightly today through the members of TRBC.

Not long after my father passed away in May 2007, TRBC once again cast a vision for global church planting. In the last year of his life, Dad often stated that he was trusting God to do greater things in the next five years of ministry than God had done in the previous fifty years. Dad had no idea when he shared those words that he would not be around to see those five years come to pass, but I firmly believe

God gave those words to him for the purpose of spurring those of us left behind to greater ministry. Further, Dad didn't develop this plan just for the sake of numbers. His desire was to raise up godly and gifted pastors who would throw caution to the wind and start churches that were aflame for Christ.

Today, Thomas Road Baptist Church has a burden to plant new churches in the Acts 1:8 mission of reaching beyond our own geographic areas to touch the world with the Gospel. We are praying that God will guide us as we seek out the right people to plant churches in many areas of need.

One of the churches that has emanated from Thomas Road Baptist Church is West Ridge Church in suburban Atlanta (see chapter 8). The pastor there is Brian Bloye, one of TRBC's former youth pastors who, as he sat under the leadership of Jerry Falwell, caught the passion for church planting and daringly serving God. On his website, Brian describes himself this way: "A church planter, pastor, husband, and father who has recklessly abandoned himself to following Jesus Christ." I find it interesting that the first words Brian uses to describe himself are "church planter." Planting churches is certainly the priority we must develop in our churches. In addition, we see through Brian's example that church planting is a contagious activity; God enabled Brian to plant a strong and vibrant church, and now Brian's great desire is to see that process continue as West Ridge plants other churches. The plan works!

In July 2007, I shared from the TRBC pulpit a new vision of planting 500 churches in the next five years. It was humbling to define this plan that originated in my father's heart. Our pastoral team prayerfully laid out the plan that would enable us to be a part of a brand-new generation of churches we envision springing to life all across this nation. That day, the plan we laid out went right back to the original vision that Dad shared with a small group of believers in that old sticky-floored Donald Duck bottling plant in 1956.

Those words and that vision came squarely from the words of Christ in Acts 1:8 (NKJV): "But you shall receive power when the Holy Spirit has come upon you; and you shall be witnesses to Me in Jerusalem, and in all Judea and Samaria, and to the end of the earth."

These words of Christ, given to the disciples who had gathered on that mountainside to witness His ascension, were the marching orders for many generations of church leaders. That short mission statement is one that we have adopted at TRBC to guide us in the area of church planting. From Acts 1:8, we have devised a four-part church planting strategy. Those four areas consist of local (Jerusalem), regional (Judea), national (Samaria), and international (the ends of the earth.) In the vision to plant 500 churches in the next five years, TRBC will be planting in areas just a few miles away from our own church campus as well as planting on the other side of the globe. In fact, as I write this chapter, TRBC has just planted four new churches in northern Iraq.

I'm sure people reading this chapter might say, "You know, our society has dramatically changed since the days of Jesus, and people simply aren't interested in church any more. So there's no need to plant new churches." I believe such thinking is erroneous. We know from studies that unchurched people are often more likely to attend new churches than they are established ones. Further, a March 2009 LifeWay Research survey of 15,000 adults found that Americans are still very willing to visit a church, especially if they receive a personal invitation. The survey found that people are most willing to hear about a local congregation through a family member's invitation (63 percent) or the invitation of a friend or neighbor who goes to the church (56 percent).

"The primary lesson North American believers should learn from this research is that many of your unchurched friends are ready for an invitation to conversation," said Ed Stetzer, director of LifeWay Research, in the report. "Unbelievers next door still need a simple, personal invitation to talk, to be in community and to church. Clearly, relationships are important and work together with marketing."

As I noted earlier in the three-part structure of how TRBC was built, the young congregation willingly joined in following the vision laid out by my father, often disregarding their personal comfort. I think that Christians today have a lot of personal comfort. We enjoy our pastor's messages, our praise and worship services, our Sunday school lessons, and the family functions at our churches, and we don't want any of it to change. But being a Christian often requires us to get out of our comfort zones. As such, we must overcome our luxury of faith in order to invite neighbors and friends and family members to church with us. Additionally, we may have to ignore our spiritual coziness by sending out key and beloved members of our churches to plant a needed new church in a neighboring community or beyond.

Summary

I want to conclude by addressing those who may be saying, "Our church does not have the resources or the wherewithal to start a new church." I would like to invite you to travel back in time for a moment to Paul's sojourn in Philippi (Acts 16).

Planting a church in this city wasn't on Paul's radar screen because he actually had no plans of going to Philippi. Then Paul experienced a vision from God wherein he saw a man from the region of Macedonia pleading with him to "come over" and "help us" (verse 9). This man can be seen today as a picture of our society that desperately needs our help. Paul, being sensitive to the Holy Spirit, immediately set off for Macedonia, and the first city he came to was Philippi. Upon arrival, Paul and Silas did not meet a lot of believers, if any—hardly the place to start a church. Nevertheless, as always, they went around sharing the truth of Jesus' resurrection and salvation through Him, even as they were seemingly in the worst place they could be. And they were actually thrown into jail, beaten, and chained up when a miraculous earthquake occurred. And through God's sovereignty, the head of the Philippi jail was saved, along with his family. Paul and Silas had not given up on God (they had been singing his praises even in jail before the holy jailhouse rock), and God had not given up on them.

Soon, Paul met a woman named Lydia, a wealthy merchant who prepared and dyed luxurious cloth, which was an expensive commodity. Only the affluent could purchase her products. This woman also became a believer in Jesus Christ through Paul's teachings. We see that God opened her heart so that she would "heed the things spoken by

Paul" (verse 14). After she was baptized, Paul stayed for a time with Lydia and her family. I'm sure this was an amazing time of spiritual growth for them all as they were able to sit at the feet of the greatest teacher of God's Word who ever lived.

Another notable convert in Philippi was a demon-possessed girl. One day, while Paul and other believers were going out to pray, they met up with this slave girl who was possessed by a demon, which gave her the power to predict the future. She began following Paul around, frequently shouting out slanderous and mocking remarks about his teachings. For some reason, Paul allowed this to go on for several days. Finally, he commanded the demon to come out of this girl, which it quickly did. It was this action that got Paul and Silas thrown into prison because this girl had been a source of income for her devious masters. When the demon was out of her, she no longer had the power of divination, causing her former handlers to take Paul and Silas before a magistrate with trumped-up charges.

And so Paul and Silas had seen three converts gloriously saved, in addition to their family members. How do we know that they were "fired-up" Christians? Ten years after their salvation experiences, a healthy church had been formed. If they had drifted away from God following their salvation, the church would not have gotten off the ground. Acts 16:40 tells us, "So they went out of the prison and entered the house of Lydia; and when they had seen the brethren, they encouraged them and departed." This is the church that Paul and Silas left behind in Philippi:

- a rich merchant (and her household)

- a jailer (and his household)

- a formerly demon-possessed girl

That's it—just a few people with colorful résumés. If this were a congregation starting out today, I doubt many people would give it much of a chance of surviving. In fact, many people would tragically write it off from the onset, forgetting that God often uses the unlikeliest of people to be His messengers. Imagine a pastor saying to you, "I just started a new church, and I'm really excited about it. Our congregation is composed primarily of a former suicidal jailer, a rich businesswoman, and a girl who was recently possessed by a demon." You would probably smile politely and think, *Man, I'll never go to that crazy church!*

Listen, when you are living out the mind of Christ as depicted in the book of Philippians and following His precepts for your life, God may place you in some unlikely territory. You might face persecution because of your Christian witness (like Paul and Silas) or feel God calling you to attend a church that isn't what you're used to (like the one at Philippi). Remember, when God is in the work, great churches will flourish in the most amazing places and through the most incredible circumstances. I think specifically of Lydia, who certainly had nothing in common with a slave girl or a tough prison jailer. But it didn't matter because the three of them were, together, the foundation of this church; their faith in Christ was their sudden bond. As Christians, our common ground is found in Christ, because in Him we are *all* equal.

Let's travel about ten years down the road to the writing of the Epistle to the Philippians so we can catch a glimpse of what was happening following the salvation experiences of this church's founding members. Look at the first verse of Philippians (NKJV) to see how the congregation had grown: "Paul and Timothy, bondservants of Jesus Christ, to all the saints in Christ Jesus who are in Philippi, with the bishops and deacons." We see that a leadership team was in place at Philippi; bishops were overseers of the church body, while deacons served the needs of the members. From its meager beginnings, this church appears to have grown into a strong and vibrant community of believers.

In the case of the church at Philippi, what started out as implausible and small grew to be great. It is time for the local church today to understand that what we need are some improbable churches to sprout up all over our nation. We need to reach and influence the lives of some improbable young men like Jerry Falwell—a onetime high school troublemaker and local star athlete who had no interest in God—who will believe in Christ, grow in Christ, and eventually take on the roles of planting churches and influencing our decaying culture. It is time for the local church to put aside comfort in order to make an impact where none is being made. I truly believe church planting is the greatest avenue by which we can win souls to Christ. It must become our passion.

The threefold mission of Thomas Road Baptist Church is to *WIN* people to Christ, help them GROW in Christ and then SEND them out for Christ! That mission statement was given by Christ Himself and is still relevant today. Today's churches must be focused on all three aspects of that mission if we truly believe we can reach the uttermost parts of the earth!

ABOUT THE CHURCH PLANTER—

Dr. Jonathan Falwell is the Senior Pastor of Thomas Road Baptist Church and Executive Vice President of Spiritual Affairs for Liberty University in Lynchburg, Virginia. He has served at TRBC under the leadership of his father, Founding Pastor Dr. Jerry Falwell, since 1995.

Jonathan earned his Bachelor of Science degree from Liberty University in 1987. He earned his Master of Arts in Religion from the Liberty Baptist Theological Seminary in 1996. He earned his law degree (Juris Doctor) in 2005 from William Howard Taft University in Santa Ana, California.

Falwell is the host of a weekly nationwide television show called *Main Street Today*. He interviews leaders from all sectors of society about their faith and how they use their faith to make a difference in our society. The Rev. Falwell has also appeared as a guest on numerous television and radio programs nationwide including *Oprah* (syndicated), CNN and the Fox News Network. He is also the author of *One Great Truth: Finding Your Answers to Life*.

Jonathan and his wife, Shari, have four children; Jonathan Jr. (born 1996), Jessica (born 1997), and Natalie and Nicholas (born 2000.) They reside in Lynchburg, Virginia.